SURVIVING ⌐TNER

⌐ⅢDOW Room

⌐attle

How To Books for General Reference

Arranging Insurance
Becoming a Father
Buying a Personal Computer
Caring for Someone at Home
Cash from Your Computer
Choosing a Nursing Home
Choosing a Package Holiday
Dealing with a Death in the Family
Having a Baby
Helping Your Child to Read
How to Apply to an Industrial
    Tribunal
How to be a Local Councillor
How to be an Effective School
    Governor
How to Claim State Benefits
How to Lose Weight & Keep Fit

How to Plan a Wedding
How to Raise Funds & Sponsorship
How to Run a Local Campagin
How to Run a Voluntary Group
How to Survive Divorce
How to Take Care of Your Heart
Living Away From Home
Making a Complaint
Making a Video
Making a Wedding Speech
Managing Your Personal Finances
Successful Grandparenting
Successful Single Parenting
Taking in Students
Teaching Someone to Drive
Using the Internet
Winning Consumer Competitions

Other titles in preparation

The How To Series now contains more than 200 titles in the following
categories:

Business & Management
Computer Basics
General Reference
Jobs & Careers
Living & Working Abroad

Personal Finance
Self-Development
Small Business
Student Handbooks
Successful Writing

Please send for a free copy of the latest catalogue for full details
(see back cover for address).

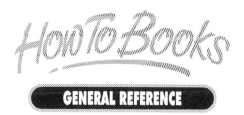

GENERAL REFERENCE

SURVIVING YOUR PARTNER

How to live with the death of the
person closest to you

Sylvia Murphy

Foreword by Katie Boyle

How To Books

British Library Cataloguing in Publication Data
A catalogue record for this book is available from the British Library.

© Copyright 1998 by Sylvia Murphy

First published by How To Books Ltd, 3 Newtec Place,
Magdalen Road, Oxford OX4 1RE, United Kingdom.
Tel: (01865) 793806. Fax: (01865) 248780.

Note: The material contained in this book is set out in good faith for
general guidance and no liability can be accepted for loss or expense
incurred as a result of relying in particular circumstances on statements
made in the book. Technical and legal matters are complex and liable to
change, and readers should check the current position with the relevant
authorities before making personal arrangements.

Produced for How To Books by Deer Park Productions.

Typeset by PDQ Typesetting, Stoke-on-Trent, Staffs.
Printed and bound by Cromwell Press, Trowbridge, Wiltshire.

Contents

List of Illustrations

Foreword

This understanding book by Sylvia Murphy strikes many chords in me – let me tell you why.

It was February 1976 and, leaving my husband, Greville, in London, I'd arrived on a working trip to Cardiff in the late afternoon. Our rehearsals were called for 8am next day so I decided to have a really early night, and after a long and happy telephone call to Greville I turned the light out at 9.30pm.

Then the telephone rang. Short persistent rings which shocked me out of the deepest sleep. I looked at my travelling clock – it glowed 4.30am. I felt sure there was some mistake, probably a misrouted early call – 'Yes?' – I must have sounded grumpy. An impersonal voice I'd never heard before asked 'Is that Miss Boyle?' and, without any further preamble said: 'I have some bad news for you. Your husband is dead.'

That was how my whole world collapsed. The shock was devastating. Suddenly I was a widow at 48 and my husband was only just 55.

The numbness was protective in the early days – but gradually, as the pain surfaced, the reality became similar to undergoing surgery without the aid of anaesthetics.

By instinct I would have gone to ground and become temporarily reclusive. But not only did I have working commitments, I also had a younger sister who flew in from our native Italy and insisted on my honouring them – even to the point of introducing a fashion show in a different town for nine whole weeks. I can remember virtually nothing of those weeks except for the warmth and understanding that came from the audiences and gave me the strength to walk on stage. This would have been the very last way I would have chosen to survive the death of my beloved husband, but in retrospect I have no doubt that I owe the most tremendous debt of gratitude to my sister and every one of my colleagues who stood by me. The importance of words played a great part in my survival.

I was still 'Dear Katie', the agony aunt of the *TV Times*, at that time, and being obliged to produce a weekly page on the subject of other people's problems was surprisingly therapeutic – especially as a lot of the readers wrote comfortingly. Again I became aware of the power of words to a widow.

I even crossed swords with a Baptist minister on this subject. He took me to task when I suggested that a young girl should 'talk' to her father who had died recently. He said that I was encouraging the youngster to 'dabble in the occult', and he added that many people suffer depression and mental illness from these supposedly 'innocent' activities!

I was so incensed by his remarks because I'd discovered only recently that one of the most painful facets of losing a loved one is the sudden silence. The loss of a familar and treasured voice. I found enormous comfort in continuing to speak openly to Greville in the happy conviction that there is an unbroken continuity of love between this world and the next. God is love and teaches us that life is everlasting – why ever should He object if we continue a terrestrially interrupted conversation? Words – always important.

I did find that time was a great ally – and whilst the vividness of my memories of that fateful night in Cardiff have never faded, the actual pain gradually dulled, and after three years I married again. A gentle, kind and wise man with whom I have now shared nearly nineteen blissfully peaceful years. We had both been widowed, but whereas Greville had died so suddenly, his wife, Ann, had been ill for a number of years and he had nursed her lovingly through an increasingly painful time.

Peter and I have often discussed whether a lingering or sudden parting is easier to cope with. We still don't know the answer, but the fact that we can talk freely on this subject reveals yet again **the importance of words** – and in different circumstances Peter and Ann felt they had been given that all important time to say to each other all they wanted to before her death.

You will find in these caring pages by Sylvia Murphy that we fully agree that there are no hard and fast 'rules' as to how best we can live on when our partner dies.

In no way can we go over, under or around the pain of parting – somehow we just have to muddle *through* as best we can, and the method depends entirely on our individual characters and the relationship we have lost. From a personal point of view, I'm sure we should never allow 'if onlys' to torture us – these are useless at best, and self-destructive at worst – and then again when the dreaded day comes, however it overtakes us, *never underestimate the importance of words.*

Sylvia has chosen many wise and helpful ones in this book.

Katie Boyle

Preface

Numerous books have been written by people whose partners have died, telling how it was for them and how they survived, all of them well worth reading. However, little is written about the practicalities of how to survive the terrible situation you find yourself in, and where you can get help other than counselling and support groups. That is what this book aims to do.

I wish it had been to hand when I was first stumbling around trying to deal with my life after my partner died. I had to be told by an official dealing with something quite different that I could apply for a widow's pension and death grant. Heaven knows what other help I missed out on through ignorance.

If you are one of those people who does not want to bring changes into their new life alone – and there are many who choose that path – this book is not for you. It is for those who want to know that they have a future apart from being 'poor so-and-so whose partner died' and who will welcome a few suggestions as to how to take some positive steps towards that future.

Sylvia Murphy

1
Meeting Bereavement

FACING THE DEATH

Feeling the pain

The emotional agony caused by the death of someone you love is hard to imagine by anyone who has never experienced it. Sometimes preparation begins early in life through the death of a friend or relative, and most people eventually have to face a parent dying.

But none of this can be compared with the devastating loss of a life partner, the person who has shared your waking and sleeping moments, your pleasures and pains, for however long a time. When that happens the agony is multiplied.

Those who have been through the experience will identify with the immediate physical reactions of choking, pains in the head and chest, sometimes a complete blackout. The sensation has been described as 'like being picked up and flung across a room, slammed against the wall'. At first you are certain that you are going to die as well, and you welcome the idea because you cannot possibly survive this awful thing that is happening. Then you realise that you won't die after all and you wish you could, because the thought of surviving alone is worse than dying.

But you do survive, almost against your will, and the next reaction is a numbness, a sense of unreality. Into this sense of unreality there intrudes, from time to time, the realisation that the most significant person in your life is no longer there, that he or she has done the unthinkable, has set off on a one-way journey without you, and you have been left alone. There is an enormous dark hole in your life. And on top of all that you are expected to pick yourself up and get on with things.

Making things more difficult

This loss can occur at any time, for any reason, in any kind of partnership. It is no easier to bear if the death was sudden or as a result of a long illness. It is no different if the partnership has been a

13

long or a short one. It is as intense for same-sex as for heterosexual relationships.

It can be made more complicated by the presence of children, or by the attitude of some people that a young person will get over the loss more easily because they are sure to meet someone else soon.

And the person who has lost a partner of the same sex may have to bear added pain through the fact that other people have not been aware of the depth of the relationship, or may have refused to acknowledge it. A family that disapproves of the partnership can sometimes be ruthless in excluding the partner at the time of death.

As well as being shut out by the family, a partner who is not the legal or named next of kin can find it very difficult to prove any right to be included in the processes surrounding a death. Homosexual partners or those in extra-marital or short-term cohabitation relationships are not recognised by the authorities as having any rights of access either to a dying person or to the dead body.

The problem can be avoided if a person has already made their own funeral arrangements or has set out their wishes in writing as a 'Living Will'. Also known as an 'Advance Directive', this sort of document normally gives instructions about such things as medical treatment and the manner of death. It can also include directives about who is to be present at their death, if at all possible, and who must be informed about the funeral. Suggested forms of wording for a Living Will can be obtained from the Terence Higgins Trust or the Natural Death Centre (see the Useful Addresses section).

While a Living Will isn't as legally binding as a Will that disposes of property, it makes it far less likely that a partner will be excluded at the end.

Seeing the body

When a death has been comparatively peaceful as the result of an illness it is quite normal for the partner who is the next of kin to be present at the end. In such a situation he or she can be left alone for a time to take leave of the loved one in privacy.

When a death has occurred suddenly, usually as the result of an accident, or in the distressing circumstances of a murder or a suicide, things become more difficult.

Identifying the body

For a start, at every death someone has to identify the body, by law. This can be the proprietor of a nursing home or a hospital official, but it is more usually the next of kin and in the case of an accident or sudden death it has to be someone who knew the victim. So the bereaved partner may have no choice but to view the body, whether they want to or not, and this is certainly not pleasant in the surroundings of a hospital morgue.

Making your choice
However, in circumstances where there is a choice, where someone else has done the formal identification, there is often conflicting opinion about whether the partner should see the body and spend time with what is left of the loved one. In the past well-meaning relatives and friends have advised against it, thinking it will increase the grief, and as a result people have said that for years they had the feeling they were still searching for the person who died.

Nowadays it is generally recognised that if the bereaved wants to see the body they should be allowed to, however bad the circumstances, and most hospitals and mortuaries are sympathetic and helpful and will do their best to make a private viewing possible. A funeral director can arrange for the body to be viewed in a Chapel of Rest, but some will make an extra charge for this.

If the bereaved feels that they can't face seeing the dead body there is no reason why they should do so. To force the issue can only add to the trauma of what is already one of the most dreadful situations anyone can find themselves in.

Registering the death
A death has to be registered before a funeral can take place. The registration must take place within five days in England and Wales, eight days in Scotland. The exceptions to this are in the case of sudden death, or death in a prison or in police custody in which case a Coroner (England and Wales) or Procurator Fiscal (Scotland) must be involved and this can hold things up.

The Registrar has to do two things:

- establish the cause of death
- establish the identity of the dead person.

To do this, a relative or some other person who was present at the death has to provide the certificate of cause of death issued by the attending doctor and, if possible, the birth and marriage certificate of the deceased, their medical card and any pension or allowance book.

The Registrar will also want to know other details such as when and where the death occurred, all the names by which the deceased

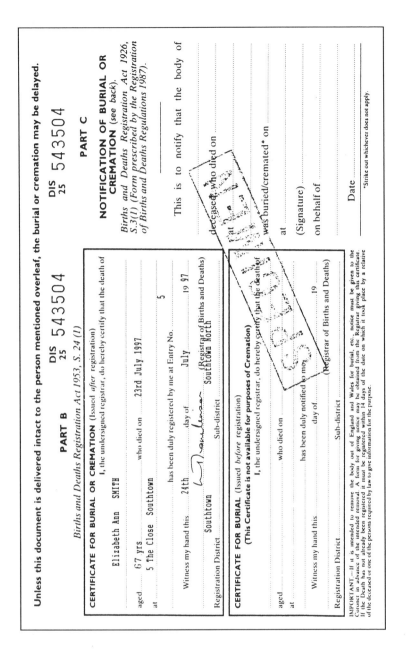

Fig. 1. Example of a Certificate for Burial or Cremation (the 'Green Form') issued by a Registrar.

16

D. Cert.

CAUTION - It is an offence to falsify a certificate or to make or knowingly use a false certificate or a copy of a false certificate intending it to be accepted as genuine to the prejudice of any person, or to possess a certificate knowing it to be false without lawful authority.

CERTIFIED COPY
Pursuant to the Births and

OF AN ENTRY
Deaths Registration Act 1953

DEATH	Entry Number	5

Registration District   Southtown   Administrative area
Sub-district   Southtown North   County of Southside

1. Date and place of death
    Twenty-third July 1997
    5 The Close   Southtown

2. Name and surname
    Elizabeth Ann   SMITH

3. Sex   Female

4. Maiden surname of woman who has married   JONES

5. Date and place of birth
    11th November 1930   Northtown

6. Occupation and usual address
    Housewife
    Wife of James Alan SMITH   Businessman
    5 The Close   Southtown

7. (a) Name and surname of informant
    James Alan SMITH

(b) Qualification
    Widower of the deceased

(c) Usual address
    5 The Close   Southtown

8. Cause of death
    I(a) Myocardial Infarction

    Certified by Z White MB

9. I certify that the particulars given by me above are true to the best of my knowledge and belief.
    James Smith

Signature of informant

10. Date of registration
    Twenty-fourth July 1997

11. Signature of registrar
    Lorraine Thomlinson Registrar

SPECIMEN

Certified to be a true copy of an entry in a register in my custody.

{ *Superintendent Registrar
{ *Registrar .... 24th July 1997 .... Date
*delete as appropriate

IAL 681880

Fig. 2. Example of a Certified Copy of an Entry in the Register (known as a 'Death Certificate') issued by a Registrar.

was known, details of occupation and previous marriages, and date of birth of any surviving widow or widower.

In most cases it falls to the surviving partner to gather all this information, make an appointment with the nearest Registrar and go along to the office. This is far from easy at a time when that person is probably walking around like a zombie with little idea of what to do next about anything, let alone legal formalities. It's important to remember that the survivor doesn't have to go through all this on their own and the support and help of a friend or relative is essential at this time.

Once the death has been registered the Registrar will issue a Certificate for Burial or Cremation (Figure 1), known as the 'Green Form' because of its colour, without which the funeral can't take place. The person registering the death can also obtain as many Certified Copies of the entry in the Register as they need, and this is the document normally referred to as the 'Death Certificate' (Figure 2).

DEALING WITH THE FUNERAL

Making arrangements
Funerals serve two purposes. The first is the practical one of disposing of a body, the second is to provide a ritual for saying farewell to the person who has died and assisting the grieving process for those who are left. Its very finality can be an added cause of distress because, in disposing of the body that has been the object of love, the bereaved is forced to face the fact that the beloved partner can never return.

Very often the surviving partner has to take the responsibility of making all the funeral arrangements, even though they are not in the best state of mind for making important decisions. Again, the support of a friend or relative can be invaluable and a good funeral director will do as much as possible to take the strain.

But even with the most competent of help, decisions will have to be made about such things as:

- whether to have a burial or a cremation

- whether to have a religious service

- where the funeral or service is to take place

- who will officiate

- how the body will be laid out
- what kind of coffin to choose
- what kind of refreshments to provide for mourners
- how to let people know about the death and the funeral
- whether to have flowers
- how much money to spend
- where to find the money.

Getting through the funeral

Once the arrangements have been made, the funeral will often go by in a blur for the bereaved partner. A sort of natural anaesthetic takes over and dulls the feelings of pain and despair so that it's possible to get through most of the ceremonial without much in the way of tears, and to acknowledge the condolences of friends and family with a brave face.

It is even possible to join in the talk afterwards about the dead person, and have a laugh about things. There's nothing heartless or shameful about this. There'll be plenty of time for tears and misery later on.

BEING LEFT ALONE

It is inevitable that when the funeral visitors have gone home the surviving partner will be left alone. It doesn't make any difference whether that person is in a house full of children, staying with friends or relatives, or physically on their own at home. Without the partner who has gone they are alone.

Then the anaesthetic begins to wear off and the real pain comes through. If there are other people around they may try to make things easier by constantly talking, by planning activities and generally trying to cheer up the suffering survivor. And out of politeness that person may respond by bottling up feelings in the belief that other people will be upset and embarrassed by an open show of grief.

This kind of situation can go on for some time before the first flood of tears breaks the emotional log jam. Whilst a bereaved person should always have a shoulder to cry on if they want it, they should also have the option of being left to let go in private.

These tears are important because without them many people

find they can't cope with their grief. However, there are people who go through a bereavement without crying at all; this doesn't mean that their feelings are less intense, simply that they have reacted in a different way.

LIVING WITH YOUR FEELINGS

Being in shock
Many people believe that because they are emotionally strong and have always been able to cope with life's difficulties, they will find it easy enough to get through the aftermath of their partner's death. The problem is that the nervous system has its own way of dealing with the resulting emotional and physical stresses and can over-ride the mental composure of the strongest of people, taking them by surprise.

Common involuntary reactions are:

- bursting into tears unexpectedly

- uncontrollable shaking

- dizzy spells

- inability to sleep

- sleeping too much

- poor concentration

- tendency to have accidents

- uncharacteristic loss of memory

- inability to make rational decisions

- inability to express your thoughts

- inability to remember where you are or what you are doing

- constantly re-living the events surrounding the death.

Added to many of these symptoms is fear because not coping is an unfamiliar experience. They know that they are showing signs of falling to pieces and they have no way of knowing how long this will last or whether they will ever get back to being their old selves.

It is easy to understand that, in this state, people shouldn't have to make major decisions about their future or anyone else's. Even more, they shouldn't have to shoulder responsibility at work while the immediate symptoms persist. Most symptoms will fade away eventually but they shouldn't be ignored.

Feeling relieved

It needs to be recognised that there are some people who don't feel any grief or loneliness after losing their partners. For some, the death is a release from a relationship that has been difficult and constricting. However, they are likely to experience the same symptoms of shock. They may also feel terrible guilt both at their lack of grief and at not having made their partner feel more valued and happy when they were alive.

People in this situation need just as much care and understanding as those who miss their partners. Their reaction may be of a different kind but it is nonetheless intense and, if wrongly handled, can affect the rest of their lives and any future relationships.

STOPPING THE CLOCK

Arresting time

Actually stopping the clock in the house at the moment of death is a symbolic action in some societies.

Metaphorically wanting to arrest time, to stay in the last day of the loved one's life, is a common reaction. Every day that passes takes the beloved further away and makes the death seem more real. It often seems preferable to stay in a fantasy world where the dead person may still recover, where the news of the death may yet turn out to be a dreadful mistake.

One of the more famous historical examples of this is Queen Victoria who, after the death of Prince Albert, ordered that none of his possessions be removed and his personal routines be continued as though he was alive. His writing desk was left as he had last used it. His valet had to lay out his night clothes, brush and prepare his day clothes as though he might suddenly need to use them again.

Few people confuse this fantasy with reality. However, it can happen that the bereaved will stay indoors indefinitely and do nothing for themselves or anyone else. They let the cobwebs spread over their homes and their lives because that's easier than making the effort to move on and rebuild their world.

Moving on

Most people will soon see that this is a waste of the rest of their life and isn't what their dead partner would have wanted for them. Just as the person who has gone has set out on a journey alone, so the one who is left must begin to travel along the road to recovery and emotional independence.

CASE STUDIES

Mary loses her lifelong partner

Mary is a spinster in her 70s. She was schoolteacher all her working life, finishing her career as a deputy headmistress in a large secondary school. When she was still a young woman she and her friend Rose, a university professor, fell in love and set up home together. Because there was a need to maintain a respectable veil over the nature of their relationship, they deliberately gave the impression that they shared a home as a matter of convenience. When Rose becomes ill with cancer Mary nurses her devotedly, staying in the hospice and sleeping at her bedside during the last weeks. Because neither of them have children there is little family help available apart from Rose's brother and his wife, but they only make one brief visit during her illness.

After Rose's death Mary feels shattered. She is constantly breaking down and crying and unable to get to grips with organising anything. At first she is relieved that Rose's brother turns up to help with registering the death and organising the funeral. However, he takes over completely without consulting Mary at all and the arrangements he makes are nothing like what Rose wanted. Mary tries to protest but is brushed aside and told it's none of her business any more.

James is released from a miserable life

James was married to Elizabeth for 50 years. She was always very dependent on him and as the years passed she became less loving and more critical of everything he did. She refused to have sex with him, but on the two occasions when he met other women he would have been happy with, she threatened suicide so that he would stay with her. After he retired she began to suffer from angina and he suspected that this was invented in order to keep him running around after her. He often imagined how peaceful life would be without her, and even fantasised about getting rid of her. When she dies suddenly of a heart attack he is thrown into terrible confusion and he can hardly believe how shocked and tearful he is. He immediately believes that in some way he has been responsible for her death.

Janet's husband meets with an accident

Janet and Leroy have been married for ten years and have two children, Sara and Robert, aged seven and five. Since Leroy lost his job two years ago, Janet, who is a senior bank clerk, has been the sole breadwinner while Leroy has looked after the children and the home. They have both been happy with this arrangement because Leroy enjoys gardening and working on home improvements. One day a police officer comes to see Janet at work and tells her that Leroy has been electrocuted whilst working on some fittings in the kitchen. A neighbour called an ambulance but Leroy was declared dead on arrival at the hospital. Janet is so stressed at the news that she faints. She is given medical care and her parents, who live about 50 miles away, are called. They come straight away and help her to deal with the necessary inquest, the registration and all the decisions about the funeral.

SUMMARY

1. Suffering the death of a partner brings the symptoms of physical as well as emotional shock.

2. Those symptoms can make you feel as though you, too, are about to die.

3. You may have to decide whether you want to see the body or not.

4. You may be expected to take responsibility for organising a funeral.

5. You will have to face up to talking to other people, who may not want to leave you alone.

6. You may find yourself excluded from the death and funeral by your partner's immediate family.

7. You may feel relieved at the death of your partner.

DISCUSSION POINTS

The discussion points at the end of each chapter aim to help you relate the subject matter to your own circumstances. Suggested ways of approaching the issues raised are given on page 100.

1.   Could you cope with the stress and pain of losing your partner?

2.   Could you face organising a funeral and attending to all the other necessary practical tasks that follow a death?

3.   If you are an 'unofficial' partner, how could you make sure of being included in the death and the funeral arrangements?

4.   Could you deal with people who are trying to· be helpful but won't leave you alone?

2
Coping with Grief

UNDERSTANDING THE PROCESS

Feeling different

The last thing anyone wants to hear in the depths of grief is that what they are going through is entirely normal, that other people have felt like that before and survived.

For the bereaved, the suffering is so shocking and so different from anything else they have experienced that it feels unique. It's sometimes insulting to be told that other people know how you feel – how can they, when this is your own personal private experience that nobody has had before and that you are coping with in your own unique way?

Following a pattern

The psychological wound caused by the loss of a loved one can be compared to a severe physical wound. It is expected to hurt and it is also expected to get better, passing through the natural stages of healing as it does so.

But no one ever completely recovers. Everyone is left with a scar that changes them in some way. Part of the process of recovering is learning to live with this scar and with the fact that there will always be days when it aches.

Some people have likened the experience to losing a limb. Eventually the wound heals over and the victim learns to manage life without the missing part, but there is always the sensation that it should be there. They are always aware that once they had the limb that has now gone for ever.

In just the same way as recovery from a physical wound can be charted, those who have studied grief in a professional capacity recognise a set pattern, a number of stages that the bereaved person has to deal with before they can come back to anything approaching normality. Briefly, these are:

1. Shock
2. Sorrow
3. Anger
4. Apathy and depression
5. Recovery.

Shock

This can take the form of both physical and emotional reactions and is shown in some or all of the symptoms described in Chapter 1. It can also include feelings of denial that the death has taken place at all, a feeling that the doctors must have made a mistake, that what is happening is all part of a dream. Sometimes the shock causes physical illness because the body's immune system can't cope with the pressure.

Sorrow

This can be an overwhelming feeling of desolation as you realise that the death must be accepted, that the dead person will never come back. It can also be mixed with feelings of guilt, usually unfounded, that the death wouldn't have occurred if only you had done this or that differently.

Anger

Sometimes this is quiet and inwardly directed, sometimes it is a desperate rage which takes the form of shouting and screaming abuse – at the dead person for having the nerve to go and leave you, at God for letting this terrible thing happen, at yourself for caring so much, at anyone else who happens to be involved and especially at anyone who is trying to help.

Apathy and depression

Just at the time when friends think you should be getting over your loss, things seem to become worse. You face the start of every day mourning the dead person and wondering if there is any point in getting out of bed. You lack interest in everything around you and feel constantly tired and depressed. You might even find yourself sinking into clinical depression and needing medical help.

Recovery

This isn't just the appearance of a return to normality, because appearances can deceive. It's the stage when you begin to feel energy and enthusiasm for new projects, when you can go for whole days at a time without thinking about your lost partner, when you can remember and talk about your partner without feelings of grief.

These are very generalised descriptions and it's important to realise that if your experiences are different, or more extreme, you aren't reacting abnormally. Some people by-pass some of the stages, others experience them all at the same time as a state of seamless chaos. The progression through them isn't necessarily neat and tidy, either. Some days it will seem that you have started to get over your loss, then another day all the early feelings will come sweeping back.

RELEASING EMOTIONS

Trying to talk

Because you have lost the person who was probably closest to you, in whom you may have confided all your deepest feelings, it will be very difficult to find outlets for releasing your pent-up emotions after the death. Talking to friends can be an option, but many people find this difficult as they are aware that they are in danger of boring or embarrassing friends and neighbours who may not be aware that they can help by just sitting and listening for an hour, without making comments or judgements.

In fact, the bereaved often find that their acquaintances avoid talking to them. Either they are afraid they may say the wrong thing or they don't have the time to lend a sympathetic ear, much as they would like to. This can only add to the difficulties of what is, for some bereaved people, an almost intolerable situation.

Writing letters

Some people get around the problem of not being able to talk to their missing partners by writing them letters. You may feel silly getting out pen and paper and pouring out your feelings into long letters that you know will never be posted, because there is nobody to read them and reply. But people who have tried this have found it a very satisfying way of working through their feelings. Some even go as far as to write imaginary replies from their partner which help them to see the situation from a fresh perspective.

Reaching a turning point

Some people find that their wounds heal slowly and gradually, others talk of reaching a turning point when they begin to put the pain behind them and open up to the world again. Turning points can be varied and unexpected. Some record the moment a new pet comes into their life and they feel able to give and receive affection once again. Some decide to go away on a journey. Some decide to go to a therapy group. Some find they are asked for help by someone in more need than they are.

One young man, planning his suicide because the pain of living without his partner was unendurable, found that the very process of making the preparations helped him to pass through his first full day without crying and this made him realise that he had a future on his own after all.

CARING FOR DEPENDANTS

Keeping going

It is difficult to give in to any release of emotion when there are young children or other dependants to care for. It's only natural in that situation to feel the need to be strong, to keep the environment as stable as possible, to provide support for those you are caring for. But if you think only of others and keep your own feelings tightly bottled up you are in danger of slowing the natural grieving process and making problems for yourself later on.

You may also make it difficult for the people you are caring for to let go and work out their own grief. Because they, in their turn, want to spare your feelings, they may feel obliged to keep theirs in check.

If what you really want to do is put your arms around other members of the family and cry on their shoulders, there is a strong possibility that they want to do the same and there is only one way of finding out. A person who has lost their partner can easily be blind to the fact that, even though their loss is different, other members of the family have also been bereaved.

Recognising your own needs

It isn't selfish to take time for yourself by finding someone else to provide substitute care for your dependants while you go out. You may want to go to the pub or the cinema, or go shopping. Or you may need to talk with a friend who can provide more neutral sympathy than family members. There may be feelings that you simply can't share with your parents or your children, such as the sexual or financial aspects of your loss, and you will find that you can face up to these problems more readily if you can discuss them with someone.

NEEDING PROFESSIONAL HELP

Getting stuck

Bottling up their feelings or being unable to talk about their loss are only two of the reasons that some people become stuck in the process of recovering from their grief. When it happens that, after several months, things don't seem to be getting any better, it's time to ask for professional help.

The symptoms of this lack of recovery vary from person to person. They can show up in any of these forms:

- increasing dependence on alcohol or drugs, either legal or illegal

- a continuing inability to cope with daily life and work

- a continuing need to weep

- an inability to sleep

- inability to shake off the feeling that life just isn't worth living

- serious thoughts of suicide.

Seeking help

It may seem that there is no way of treating these symptoms of intense grief because the only apparent treatment, of having your loved one back again, is impossible.

A visit to your GP may result in a prescription that treats the symptoms but does nothing to relieve the underlying cause of the problem. Or it may lead to sympathetic and understanding professional counselling from a practice counsellor.

You may want to make your own approach to one of the organisations that specialise in bereavement counselling. Bereavement counsellors are trained not only in counselling but also in the specialised understanding of grief and the possible complications you may face.

They have a good record of helping even those who have been in the depths of depression to become fit and well and able to get on with their lives.

LEARNING TO LIVE AGAIN

The first time that you wake in the morning on your own with a cheerful heart and look forward to the coming day will be the first day when you realise that you are going to be able to live again in the fullest sense of the word. In some ways, this is the biggest change that will affect you after your bereavement, yet it is the one that you can't plan for or bring about by your own actions.

This experience doesn't mean that you are beginning to forget your dead partner. It does mean that you are learning to live with the pain of your loss and that you know you have a future waiting for you.

CASE STUDIES

Mary is isolated

Although many friends from the past come to the funeral Mary feels totally alone with her grief because she can't talk about her true feelings for Rose. After the funeral and the unpleasant problems with Rose's brother, Mary is relieved to be left on her own. She begins every day by weeping and wondering if it's worth getting up to begin the day. She finds herself talking to Rose as she goes about the house and she often forgets that Rose is dead and wonders why she's late coming home. She feels embarrassed when she has to go out because she's sure people notice that she looks ill and her eyes are always red and swollen.

As the days turn into weeks and the pain doesn't ease, she feels that she can't carry on alone and she begins to plan her suicide, knowing that nobody will be too upset over it. Then she receives a phone call from an ex-student of Rose's, Josephine, who wants Mary to help her to research and write a biography of Rose. Mary welcomes the idea and makes an appointment to see Josephine.

James is haunted

James tries to pull himself together after Elizabeth's funeral. He would like to make the most of the last years of his life and he continues to see his friends regularly, particularly at the local garden club, and generally gives the impression that he is making a good recovery. But however busy he makes himself he can't throw off feelings of guilt and disloyalty towards Elizabeth and increasingly he feels that she is haunting the house, criticising everything he does. His guilt is now mixed with feelings of rage at Elizabeth, sure that she only died as a final master-stroke to make him miserable. He begins to suffer physical symptoms such as abdominal cramps and headaches and he goes to see his GP. The doctor diagnoses acute stress brought on by his guilt feelings over Elizabeth's death and recommends that he contact Cruse Bereavement Care to ask for counselling.

Janet keeps going

Janet's parents are very supportive and want to continue to help her after the funeral. They try to persuade her to move back to live with them, but Janet likes her job and her independence. After her first display of shock she shuts away her feelings because she thinks it will be bad for the children to see her crying and moping about. As soon as the funeral is over she makes arrangements with a friend to meet the children from school every day and goes back to work.

SUMMARY

1. Grief follows a set pattern but everyone experiences this differently.

2. Grieving people need to be able to express their emotions.

3. People often bottle up their grief for the sake of those around them.

4. Grieving people should recognise their own needs as well as those of others.

5. People often reach unexpected turning points in their recovery from their loss.

6. People who get stuck in the grieving process may benefit from professional counselling.

DISCUSSION POINTS

1. How could you help a friend who is grieving for their partner?

2. What could you do if you suspect that a member of your family is bottling up grief in order not to upset you?

3. Could you plan the turning point in the recovery of a friend?

4. Could you persuade a friend to ask for the help of a bereavement counsellor?

3
Becoming a Single Parent

If your partner has died young, the chances are that after the death you will be left with children to bring up on your own. They may be:

- children you had in your relationship with your deceased partner

- your children from a previous relationship

- your partner's children from a previous relationship

- some combination of all three.

However your joint parental responsibility came about, when the partner with whom you were sharing the parenting dies you become a single parent and from the very first you will find yourself facing alone the situations and decisions that you used to share with your partner.

EXPLAINING THE SITUATION

The first hurdle will be explaining to the children what has happened, what is happening and what is going to happen in the near future. However frightening it is for them, shutting them out will only make things worse.

But explanations must take into account what the children can understand about death and this depends very much on their age and their previous experience.

Understanding children's reactions

As a general rule, age-related reactions will be as follows:

- **Little babies** will only miss a parent if there is nobody else to provide warmth, food and love. Explanations are pointless because the baby won't understand. These will come much later as the child grows up.

- **Older babies and toddlers** will realise that a parent has gone away but can't grasp the idea of that person never coming back. They will probably fret and pine for the missing parent and it's important to give them security and stability. Questions should be answered truthfully because if you explain the death by telling fairy tales the child may think you have lied when, later, he or she is old enough to understand the truth.

- At **nursery school age**, children will begin to meet with the idea of death through stories or the death of pets and they will have a strong curiosity about it. However, they will still find it very hard to grasp the fact that a dead person can't come back. They will be able to feel sorrow as they miss the presence of the dead parent, and rejection and guilt growing out of the belief that the dead parent can't have loved them, or went away because they were naughty. Once again, routine, love and reassurance are very important.

- **Infant school children** are usually beginning to understand that the dead person can't come back, but they will still feel guilt and rejection. They will also have a tendency to fantasise about the dead parent, building up mental pictures of him or her as far more perfect than they really were, and blaming the remaining parent for not living up to this fantasy. They will need opportunities to talk about their bereavement to trusted adults or to other children in the same situation. However, because children at this age are conformists and don't like to be singled out, they may resent the subject being brought up in front of a group of friends or classmates.

- **Junior school children** will have a far more realistic understanding of death and its implications. Their grieving patterns will begin to be more like those of an adult, though they will show different ways of expressing their rage and depression and may lose interest in school work and social activities. As with younger age groups, they need the security of love and affection. They also need the opportunity to talk but they don't want to have it forced upon them.

- During the **teens** the grief reactions will be similar to those of an adult but will be compounded by the normal teenage problems associated with emotional and physical development – insecurity, self-doubt, rebellion. In some families teenagers may find themselves expected to play the role of surrogate partner as the remaining parent recovers from the bereavement, which can impose an intolerable strain. At the age when it's often difficult to confide in a parent, the grieving teenager desperately needs some confidante of their own age or older.

Recognising other symptoms

In addition to the age-related reactions, children of any age will suffer agonising insecurity as they absorb the idea that if one parent can die, so can the other, and if that happens they will be left alone with no one to look after them.

For younger children this insecurity may cause:

- thumbsucking
- wetting and soiling
- refusal of food
- clinging
- whining
- temper tantrums.

For older children:

- bedwetting
- apathy
- falling behind with school work
- truancy
- theft
- vandalism
- bad temper
- rudeness
- depression.

These lists can be open-ended and, in effect, any attention-seeking behaviour may be a symptom of grief, a reaction to feeling pushed out at the time of the parent's death.

HELPING CHILDREN TO GRIEVE

Excluding the children

Children are often called the 'forgotten mourners'. Families often make the mistake of excluding them from the trauma surrounding a death and a funeral. Either they are considered to be in the way, or it is thought to be bad for them to witness the grief and bewilderment of the adults around them. They may be rushed off to stay with helpful relatives or friends until the funeral is over.

This course of action may make life easier for the bereaved adults but it denies the children an important stage in the process of leave-taking of the dead parent. As a result young children may be left feeling even more bewildered and older children pushed out and unwanted. However difficult it may seem at the time, giving children a role in the processes surrounding the death, including the funeral, can go a long way towards underpinning their feelings of security and the unity of a family.

After that, understanding that they have feelings of grief just as intense as yours, and sharing your grieving processes with them will help them towards acceptance.

Informing other significant adults

Remember that you are not the only person in your children's lives who will be able to help them forward. As soon as possible after the death you should inform the children's school and the adults organising any group they belong to. Tell them, too, exactly what the child has been told and what their reaction has been.

After that, tell the parents of the child's friends, and other members of your family – anyone who may be in a position to spend time with the child. This may prevent confusing messages and information getting across which would undermine the child's confidence about the situation.

FUNCTIONING AS A SINGLE PARENT

When you are forced to assume the role of a single parent you will find that your status in society will change overnight.

Some or all of the following will soon become obvious:

- Your children's school(s) may imply that any difficulties with work or behaviour are due to your single status.

- If you are employed your employer may imply that you are expected to work harder than other people to make up for the times when you may need to take time off to care for your children, even if you use a competent child-minder.

- If you are unemployed the Benefits Agency will imply that you should be trying to find work, even if you regard looking after your family as a full-time job.

- Friends and family will soon begin to hint that you should be looking for another partner, for the sake of the children.

It goes without saying that all of these attitudes should be strenuously resisted. But resistance isn't so easy when you are tired, lonely, vulnerable, overworked and probably short of money. It's very easy to begin to feel as though you really are a burden to society, even a scrounger, when in fact you are probably working twice as hard as the average parent and certainly contributing to society by bringing up future taxpayers.

Lastly, entering into a new relationship just to have someone to look after the children is unfair to yourself, to the children and, most of all, to the other person concerned.

BEING TWO PARENTS

One of the greatest problems faced by a single parent is just that – being the only one around. One mother who was desperately trying to compensate after the death of her partner recalls believing that she had to try to be perfect because she was the only one around.

While it is possible to single-handedly bring in enough money, provide the necessary love and attention, do all the shopping, cooking, cleaning and washing, it is no easy matter being solely responsible for the discipline and personal development of your children.

In a two-parent family there is always someone to act as backstop or counterbalance. This may involve backing up some ruling about going out with friends, staying up late, spending extra money. Or it may involve the careful reconsideration of a hasty decision about the settlement of a family dispute, or allowing the child a little more freedom than previously.

If there is another parent or significant adult around for the child to go to and pour out insecurities and resentments, this can act as an important natural safety valve. If a child with only one parent comes into conflict with that parent, the child can suddenly feel very isolated and insecure.

As a single parent, understanding all this, you may end up over-compensating in both material and emotional matters. But however hard you try to be all things to your children, you will never succeed. The best you can do is to let them feel secure in the knowledge that, however unpopular your decisions may be, you have their best interests at heart.

FINDING SUPPORT

Contacting helpful organisations

No single parent has to struggle alone. Organisations exist to provide emotional and practical support for the one-parent family, and for parents in general.

The **National Council for One Parent Families** is a registered charity working to help lone parents. It provides excellent information documents and campaigns on behalf of one-parent families.

Gingerbread is another charity which campaigns and offers help and advice. It supports over 200 local self-help groups and runs forums and training events, and publishes a quarterly newsletter.

Also, **Parentline** and the **Parent Helpline** both provide information for all parents about the help available for them.

Working parents having difficulty finding care for their children before and after school, and during the holidays, can contact the **Kids Club Network** for information about local provision, which will also include transporting the children between the club and their school.

For the addresses of all these organisations, see Useful Addresses.

Going on holiday

Even if you want to give family holidays a miss after your bereavement, you may soon become aware that your children are feeling let down when their friends talk about going away on package holidays or camping trips. Before long, if you can possibly afford it, you will be thinking of taking them away.

But where can you go without being surrounded by other families with two parents, reminding you of all that you and your children have lost with the death of your partner? How will you be able to manage, being the only person around to keep an eye on the children? What will you do in the evenings when the children have gone to bed and other couples are dining and dancing together?

You may find that it's necessary to learn to live with this but it will be easier if you talk it over with the children beforehand, warn them what the situation may be, that they will face difficult questions from other curious children, and give them ideas about how to cope with this.

Teaming up with another family

There are single parent families that come together year after year for the pleasure and convenience of holidaying as a unit. They don't want to spend the remainder of the year together but going on holiday together means there is always someone else around to help and to spend the evenings with.

The organisation **Holiday Care Service** (see Useful Addresses) provides a guide to holidays for one-parent families throughout Europe. It also publishes a guide to trusts and funds where those who would have difficulty paying for a holiday can apply for financial help.

BALANCING NEEDS

Remembering your own needs
So far in this chapter the emphasis has been on the needs of the children but it's important to remember that nobody can be a good parent if they neglect their own needs. Your children are important to you, but you are twice as important to them because you are their source of security, both physical and emotional. You are their buffer between the big hostile world and their ability to survive.

Taking care of yourself
Therefore you must take care of yourself. Your health, both mental or physical, is vitally important to your children's well-being. Not for you the indulgence of missing meals, moping around an unkempt home, getting drunk because there is nobody to care what happens to you. Your children care.

If you are ill, who will look after them? If you are drunk, who will help with their homework? If you don't clean the house, might they not become ill?

Needing your own social life
If you are conscientious and always on duty as a parent, you may find yourself becoming stale and frustrated. Whilst for some parents outings with the children and doing things around the home may be a fulfilling way of life, others may miss going out with their friends, going to clubs and classes, just interacting socially with other adults. And because they miss these things, they may feel guilty that their children are not providing all the interest they need. The idea of leaving them with a baby-sitter, of not spending every possible moment with them, may be difficult to admit. That can easily lead to parents blaming their children for their own dissatisfaction and frustration, which isn't fair on anyone.

There are ways of combining baby-sitting with friends so that you can go out and leave the children feeling secure. You may have relatives close by who can help out.

Life is never going to get back to the way it was before your partner died, but it is possible to find new balances between the demands of your family and your own personal needs.

CASE STUDY

Janet tries to manage

Janet finds that there's more to being a single parent than she thought. She reacts to any little criticism from the children that she's not doing things the way their father used to, and tries to make things as perfect as possible for them. She is therefore upset to learn that Sara is withdrawn and uncommunicative in school and Robert has started throwing tantrums and spoiling other children's work. She visits the school and talks to the teachers and a school counsellor, and they agree on a strategy for encouraging the children to talk about their father's death and to ask questions.

Just as things are settling down, Janet's friend tells her that she isn't able to take care of the children after school on a regular basis and there also looms the problem of the school holidays. Janet begins to think that she may have to move back to live with her parents after all. Then someone at work tells her about the National Council for One Parent Families and from them she finds out about Kids Clubs Network. To her relief she finds there's a club operating at one of the local schools, and her children will be met from their school and taken there in the afternoons. At first they don't like the arrangement and make a fuss about going, but Janet explains to them that she needs their help in order to manage without their father and before long they settle down.

SUMMARY

1. Children of different ages will have different reactions to the death of a parent.

2. Children will often show symptoms of disturbance and insecurity as part of their grieving process.

3. As far as possible children should be included in the funeral and other arrangements after the death.

4.   Children should be told the truth about a parent's death.

5.   Single parents don't have to struggle along without support and help.

6.   Single parents should look after themselves as well as their children.

DISCUSSION POINTS

1.   Is it fair to try to make a child understand that a dead parent will never come back again?

2.   Should a single parent try to find a partner as soon as possible?

3.   Is it fair for single parents to think about having a social life of their own?

4
Living Alone

GETTING USED TO BEING ALONE

If you have no children, or none still living at home, and your household was composed simply of yourself and your partner, your problems are going to be centred around living alone.

After the shock of the death, the upheaval and fuss of the funeral, the well meaning presence of friends and relatives, you may feel a tremendous sense of relief when you finally manage to shut the front door and be alone for the first time. As last you have time to weep in private, at last you can just sit and go over the events surrounding the death without interruption. You can wander around the place you shared together and bring back memories at will. You can, at last, begin to establish a circle of peace around the memories of your dead partner.

You can eat or not eat, have a drink or a smoke, look at photograph albums, weed the garden, watch television, read a book, play music, have a conversation with your departed partner, or simply do nothing at all, and nobody will object or try to distract you. Your time is your own.

Facing the emotional problems

Of course, that's not what you really want. You want your time to be your own to share with your partner again. You want to do the things you used to do at home together, to relax, make love, have rows, talk, laugh, be nice to each other, make each other miserable – you want it to be like it was. But that's an impossibility and you have to get used to living alone.

Even if life was hell with your partner, if the death was a release for both of you, you will find this feeling of aloneness strange to cope with at first. If you had a close and loving relationship it will be overwhelming and chaotic. A great many strange and unfamiliar emotions will come pouring in and the chances are that you'll feel very frightened and disorientated.

JANET & LEROY'S HOUSEHOLD CHECKLIST

BANK

Bank name and address ...... *EASTERN BANK – 6, HIGH STREET* ......

Bank Code...... *00–XX–XX* ......   Account number *12345678* ......

Account Name(s) ...*JAMES SMITH* ......

Joint or sole account ...*SOLE* ......

Standing orders and direct debits: Monthly   Annual

COUNCIL TAX £52 HOUSE INSURANCE £198

MEDICAL INS. £85 RAC £45

CAR INS. £30

ELECTRICITY £35

H.P. £26

CAR

Services due...*FEB – AUG* ......   Tax due...*SEPTEMEBER* ......

Garage ...*FRED'S – TEL:* ......

Insurance company ...*FAST CALL – TEL:* ......

Insurance renewal date...*31 AUG* ......   How much *APPROX £350 ANNUALLY* ......

MOT due ...*AUGUST* ......

APPLIANCES

WASHING MACHINE   Instructions *IN FOLDER IN BOTTOM DRAWER OF DESK* ......

Service details *CONTRACT X0456 TEL:* ......

CENTRAL HEATING   Programming instructions *BOTTOM DRAWER OF DESK* ......

Service details *BRITISH GAS. JULY. THEY CONTACT US.* ......

TV & VIDEO   Instructions *BOTTOM DRAWER OF DESK* ......

Breakdown service...*PETE'S TV, HIGH STREET. TEL:* ......

Licence due *FEB* ......   How much *£89.50* ......

COMPUTER   Instructions *BOTTOM DRAWER OF DESK* ......

Breakdown service...*MICROSERVICE, HIGH STREET. TEL:* ......

Fig. 3. Example of a household checklist.

HOME

Mortgage or Rent When to pay *MONTHLY* ....

Where to pay *DIRECT DEBIT FROM BANK* ....

How much ... *£210* ....

Council Tax When to pay *1ST OF MONTH APRIL TO FEB* ....

Where to pay *COUNCIL OFFICES* ....

How much .... *£52* ....

Electricity When bills arrive *QUARTERLY* ....

How to pay *MONTHLY STANDING ORDER* ....

How much ... *£35* ....

Fuse box, meter and master switches *IN FRONT PORCH* ....

Gas When bills arrive *QUARTERLY* ....

How to pay *CHEQUE TO BRITISH GAS* ....

How much *APPROX £80 PER QUARTER* ....

Meter and stop tap *CUPBOARD UNDER STAIRS* ....

Telephone When bills arrive *QUARTERLY* ....

How to pay *CHEQUE TO BRITISH TELECOM* ....

How much .... *£55 APPROX PER QUARTER* ....

Water When bills arrive *ANNUALLY – MARCH* ....

How to pay *CHEQUE TO WATER COMPANY* ....

How much .... *£250 APPROX* ....

Meter and stopcock *IN GARAGE* ....

Insurance When to renew *ANNUALLY – JULY* ....

How to renew *THEY CONTACT US WITH QUOTATION* ......

How much .. *APPROX £198 BY DIRECT DEBIT* ....

Hire Purchase What for *WASHING MACHINE* ....
or Credit

When due *MONTHLY – 5TH* ....

How to pay *DIRECT DEBIT* ....

How much *£26* ....

Electrician *JOE BLOGGS TEL:* .... Plumber *FRED BLOGGS TEL:* ....

Rubbish *PUT BY GATE ON TUESDAY MORNINGS, QUERIES TEL:* ....

Fig. 3. (continued).

You'll wake up in the morning with no one there when you open your eyes. There will be no one to touch, no one to greet, no one to share the bathroom with, to plan the day with. Every day the first thought in your head will be your lonely state and you'll wish you'd stayed asleep, and wonder if it's worth bothering to get up and get dressed. And each morning you will mourn afresh. If you are a weeper you will start each day with another cry even though your sore eyes feel as though they could never shed another tear.

Learning to live with the pain
You are going to have to get used to this, one morning at a time, and gradually you will learn to live with the pain.

And one morning you'll wake up and you'll be able to start the day without grieving, and you'll know you've taken an important step forward. That doesn't mean that every day will be as good – you'll go back many times to your original state of misery. But it does mean that it's possible not to be filled with despair and you'll want to hang on to that.

Dealing with practical matters
There will be practical matters that you have to take charge of almost immediately. Whilst you will have choices about how and when you do these things, you will have to face up to taking on all the aspects of household management that you relied on your partner to look after. It's a good idea for couples to compile a household checklist before a disaster strikes so that whoever is left has a handy guide to the things that need to be done (see Figure 3).

For example, do you know:

• when the Council Tax needs paying

• how often the bills come in and how much they are

• what credit agreements you have to pay

• what times the supermarket opens and closes

• how to work the washing machine

• how to work the central heating system

• how to programme the video recorder

- when the rubbish is collected

- where the stopcocks are for the water and gas

- where the fuse box and electricity meter are?

Do you always remember:

- to lock the back door at night

- to feed the cat or the goldfish

- to buy fresh milk

- to turn off the lights when you go out

- to wash the tea towels?

Getting to grips with practical things like these will seem incredibly important after the death, even though they may be trivial in the context of your loss. It's amazing what you can forget when you're trying to get used to managing on your own. Writing lists can help the memory. One such list, sellotaped to the hall mirror in the house of a newly-bereaved widow, read:

Patio doors?
Windows?
Cats?
Car keys?
House keys?
Purse?
Shopping list?
Work notes?
And where am I going?

Eventually you'll be remembering it all as a matter of course and the realisation that you can manage by yourself is often one of the important turning points along the road to recovery.

ESTABLISHING NEW ROUTINES

Finding advantages
Little by little you will find advantages to being alone.

- You will gradually stop eating the things you never really liked but put up with because your partner liked them.

- You will always be able to watch what you want to on the television.

- You will be able to go out without checking first if it's all right with someone else.

- You will be able to re-decorate a room the way you really want it.

- You can re-arrange the furniture or the way you use the rooms to suit your own pattern of living.

- It won't matter if you miss your regular cleaning or laundry routines or leave the sink full of dirty dishes.

All these things may sound selfish but life with another person is made up of countless tiny compromises and you are going to have to gradually unravel all those compromises so that you can emerge again as yourself.

Changing routines – going to bed

If starting the day alone sounds like the most difficult thing you will have to face, going to bed alone at night is a close second, so this is one of the routines it's sensible to change as soon as you can. There are many ways of doing this:

- Change your bedtime, making it earlier or later than it used to be.

- Give yourself something to do when you get to bed, like watching television or reading books or magazines.

- Start a course of study and do your reading last thing at night – some people find that studying is the quickest way to induce sleep!

- If you have a pet that used to be banished from the bedroom, change the rules and let them in, let them sleep on the bed. You will value the company, and so will they. (Never forget that a pet will also miss the person who has died.)

Changing routines – starting the day

Different going to bed routines will gradually bring on different waking routines:

- If the cat or the dog is there, you can begin the day with a stroke or a cuddle.

- If you've been studying, you can begin by recalling what you read the night before.

- If you need to hear a human voice, arrange for an alarm call just before your own alarm goes off, or switch on the radio first thing.

- If you used to begin the day by sharing a companionable cup of tea with your partner, change to orange juice and keep it in the fridge so that you have to get up to get at it.

All these changes can be made gradually. The object is not to sweep away the old life you used to live with your partner but to help yourself to get used to the new one that has been forced upon you.

DEALING WITH INTERFERENCE

Everyone left on their own to mourn must welcome the help and support of family, friends and neighbours. But there is often a fine line between support and interference. If your next door neighbour brings around a meal for a few days after you've been left on your own, that's helpful. If he or she is still insisting on feeding you weeks later and on top of that beginning to make you feel you should do something in return, that's interference.

If your in-laws offer to take the children away for a short holiday while you settle back to work, that's helpful. If they start nagging you to move in with them, that's interference.

If a friend drops in a leaflet about an activity or group you might join, that's helpful. If he or she turns up on the doorstep to take you along to the group, that's interference.

Distinguishing between help and interference

As a general rule of thumb, you can recognise interference because instead of feeling grateful you feel irritated and uncomfortable with what is being suggested or offered. The trouble is, the bereaved person is often feeling too low to take a firm stand, or doesn't want to offend someone who is only, after all, trying to help.

You can either defend yourself by making excuses or by stating outright that you don't want any help. Either way, you may cause offence but one of the advantages of being newly bereaved is that it gives you an excuse to behave in what may seem to be an anti-social way. You can always explain and make amends later, when you feel better about it all.

DEALING WITH FEAR

Even the strongest person is conscious of a range of new fears when they start to live alone. These are difficult to dismiss as irrational because they are founded in very real possibilities.

For example, there may be:

- Fear of losing what you have left. You have already lost your beloved partner – might you not come home one day and find that some further catastrophe has struck and your pet is dead, or your home burnt down?

- Fear of being burgled or attacked in your home. People in the neighbourhood know you are now on your own and that makes you more vulnerable to a break-in, or a visit by con artists.

- Fear of falling ill and being unable to call for help.

- Fear of dying and not being found for days.

Any of these things can happen to people who live alone and the only way you can lessen the chances of them happening to you is to take sensible precautions, which might include:

- Always checking that gas and electric appliances are turned off at night and before you go out.

- Always using a fireguard if you have an open fire.

- Closing the door of any room that contains dangers to your pet and making sure that high windows are closed.

- Locking up thoroughly at night and when you go out.

- Having a chain fitted to your front door and using it at all times.

- Leaving lights on when you'll be out after dark or buying timer plugs so that a couple of lamps will switch themselves on and off while you are out.

- Coming back to your front door with your keys ready in your hand so that you can open up and get in quickly.

- Never letting a stranger into your home unless you have made an appointment for a service agent and they can produce an identity card.

- Getting into the habit of talking to people every day, either a neighbour, the postman or a local shopkeeper, or chatting to a friend on the phone.

In the end, common sense tells us that everyone faces the chance of some kind of disaster striking in life and if we all went about our daily business worrying obsessively about it life might grind to a standstill. Government statistics say that 35 per cent of people are the victims of crime at some time or another but remember that this means it will never happen to 65 per cent of us.

CASE STUDIES

Mary buries herself in work

Mary and Josephine get on well together and Mary is soon spending long hours at the university library reading about the early background to Rose's studies and research. She takes piles of books and papers home with her each day and always settles down to read in bed each evening, which seems to bring Rose closer at this most difficult time of the day. She discovers that Josephine is lonely, living away from her parents for the first time in her life, and begins to invite her home for lunches and walks at the weekends.

James struggles on his own

James isn't sure about seeing a counsellor. He doesn't relish the thought of bringing his feelings about Elizabeth into the open with a stranger and he thinks he ought to be strong enough to manage on his own. So he does nothing about it. In spite of trying to organise himself properly, he finds it difficult to cope with the shopping and the laundry. He forgets to buy milk, but buys far too many biscuits and frozen peas. He can't get the hang of the temperature control on the washing machine and shrinks some underwear and his favourite sweater. He is alarmed to realise that he often goes to bed without locking up properly, even though that was his responsibility when Elizabeth was alive. He starts making lists to help him to remember everything (Figure 4). His headaches and cramps continue.

GOING OUT

Have I locked the windows?
Have I locked the back door?
Have I turned off the cooker?
Have I put the answerphone on?
Have I changed my shoes?
Have I got my shopping list?
Have I got my wallet?
Have I got the keys?
Am I walking or going by car?

Fig. 4. James' 'going out' memory list.

SUMMARY

1. It can be a relief for a bereaved partner to be left alone to grieve in peace.

2. It can be very difficult to adjust to life without your partner.

3. Sometimes well-meaning help can begin to seem like interference.

4. Sensible precautions should be taken against accidents or break-ins.

DISCUSSION POINTS

1. Could you judge whether a bereaved friend is ready to be left on their own?

2. What sort of memory list would you need to make?

3. How can you change your home and its routines without feeling you are trying to push your partner aside?

5
Suffering Sexual Loss

NEEDING SEX

Feeling desperate

Sex may not be your first priority when trying to adjust to life without your partner but it can be enormously important. The notion of a life's partner assumes a physical relationship and when your partner dies your own sexuality doesn't die with him or her. Even people with low sex drives speak about experiencing an almost overwhelming and quite inappropriate rush of sexual desire in the first chaos of grief.

This may be because:

- in a stable partnership, sex is associated with security and that has been wrenched away

- there is a heightened awareness of what has been lost, never to be found again

- there is a feeling of panic about the possibility of never having sex again.

Others feel the return of sexual appetites only slowly, as their grieving proceeds, but they still have to face up some time to the sense of insecurity brought on by the loss of physical love.

Feeling wanted

For many people, feeling that they are sexually attractive is part of their sense of self-worth and when the person who admired them and wanted them the most is suddenly taken away it can be a devastating blow to their self-esteem. People with healthy sex drives become used to being loved, being admired, being caressed and cuddled, enjoying the sexual act with someone whose body is as familiar to them as their own. To lose all this is a terrible deprivation and however much their minds and hearts tell them that sex is no longer important now that their loved one has gone, their bodies tell them differently.

This is just one more problem amongst all the others to be dealt with and it can't be dismissed as something that doesn't really matter. For someone already struggling in a pit of despair, a new sexual relationship is an essential part of finding themselves as a person again.

REACTING IN DIFFERENT WAYS

People respond to this sexual need in different ways:

- Some people will have ceased being sexually active long before losing their partner and they will tell themselves that as they have been without sex for so long it isn't going to bother them now.

- Some people, although they enjoyed a good sexual relationship with their partner, tell themselves that they have reached a stage in their lives when it is possible, if not desirable, to do without sex in the future.

- Some people, however strong their physical feelings, enter a period of celibacy because they can't begin to contemplate having another sexual relationship.

- Some people will be desperate for sexual release and, in the early days before it's possible to form a new long-term relationship, will take advantage of any and every offer that comes their way.

- Some people will be desperate for reassurance that someone cares about them, and will also take advantage of whatever is available.

- Some people, desperate for sex but not for the complications of a relationship, will find release in masturbation.

- Some people, desperate for either sex or reassurance but not wanting to contemplate promiscuity, will try to form a relation-ship with a new partner as soon as possible.

Looking for solutions

So many people have written and talked about a period of almost frenzied sexual activity after a partner's death that it has to be taken seriously, it isn't a figment of a few overheated imaginations.

Shocking as it may seem to some people, many feel comforted by a passionate one night stand even before the funeral has taken place. Many say they would never have got through the problems following their bereavement if they hadn't had a sexually loving friend at hand.

There are obvious dangers attached to this kind of behaviour. There are those who find themselves unwittingly becoming tangled up in unsuitable relationships as a result of post bereavement sex, and don't know how to free themselves once the relationship stops working.

Others who would like to make the new relationship permanent find themselves dumped because the other person doesn't feel the same. This is a risk that goes with any tentative new relationship, but on top of the trauma of bereavement this can be like a second kick in the teeth, twice as devastating to a person who is trying to pull themselves up after the first blow.

Waiting a 'decent interval'

Some people prefer to wait for what is known as a 'decent interval' before allowing themselves a sexual relationship. But what is a 'decent interval' and who decides it? It's a social convention, a period of time that can vary according to whoever is making the judgement. It should mean a length of time to mark respect for the dead person, or for the feelings of the bereaved, but it's more often used to pass judgement on those who don't observe 'decent' intervals and are thus thought to have done something 'indecent'.

What is certain is that people have said that the longer they leave it, the more difficult they find it to start having sex again. They lose their sexual confidence and are so consumed with doubts about whether they will be good enough in bed that they avoid the situation altogether, forgetting that the other person concerned is probably equally afraid.

Discovering self-release

Self-release, or masturbation, is a little-discussed alternative to having sex with other people, yet many people of both sexes say they find it a very satisfactory way of dealing with the loss of a sex life.

There has always been a tendency to regard any form of masturbation as something dirty and unnatural, even dangerous, only resorted to by those who can't find a sexual partner.

The fact is that it is often preferred by people who don't want to find a sexual partner, who would rather be self-sufficient. It is neither dirty nor dangerous – it's a lot safer than any other form of sexual activity as it can neither spread infection nor cause pregnancy. Nor can it result in painful emotional entanglements. And there is nothing unnatural about it, since, for both men and women it is giving the same kind of physical stimulation as any other kind of sexual activity.

BEING AVAILABLE

Taking advantage

There is another side to the discussion of sexual activity – where does it all come from? Some people may have read the first part of this chapter and be thinking 'If only...'.

But many of those who have been through the situation will recognise the fact that, almost overnight, people's attitudes change after a partner has died. They have quickly had to get used to the fact that, even if they didn't regard themselves as available, other people did. There were plenty of people, sometimes in the most unexpected quarters, ready to take advantage of their tragedy.

Changing perceptions

It may only be a few days after the death when the hints begin. A neighbour or the partner of a friend will say something like 'Is there anything I can do to help you? Please don't hesitate to ask...' and the way it is said destroys the apparent neutrality of the words.

Or someone will bring tasty little meals around to your home, will hang around while you eat, fussing, washing up, dropping hints like 'I've always admired the way you...' or 'You must miss so-and-so very much – I'll do anything I can to help you get over it.'

Or you may go out for a comforting drink or cup of coffee with a group of friends who well know your situation and find yourself the subject of suggestive physical contact from someone you never thought might be attracted to you.

These approaches can come as a shock and you can either take advantage of them or ignore them according to your own feelings. You may choose to freeze out the person concerned. Maybe you don't like the thought of sexual deception or you don't like the though of sex itself at the moment and you are sure that you will find more acceptable opportunities in the future.

But often they aren't unwelcome because there is always a certain thrill in realising that you are desirable to someone, whoever they are. And if you are taking up an offer from someone else's partner it's a safe bet that they won't want any more than a passing sexual encounter, that you are free from the danger of further unwanted entanglement.

FEELING GUILTY

A person grieving for a dead sexual partner is inevitably going to feel horrible pangs of guilt as they admit to themselves that they need to have sex with someone else. This guilt may increase when they find someone else they fancy and then later admit that they have enjoyed the experience.

There will be even more reason for guilt if the person providing the sexual comfort was the partner of a friend or neighbour. In this case the guilt may well be mixed with regret about behaviour that they would have avoided in normal circumstances.

Whatever the source of the guilt, it's a natural emotion, not one that should become overwhelming. It shouldn't stop people from learning to manage life on their own, or from being able to settle down to a steady relationship with someone new.

The ultimate test of whether it's reasonable to feel guilty is to ask yourself two questions:

1. Do you really believe that your partner wouldn't have wanted you to enjoy a sexual relationship with anyone else?

2. What do you think he or she would be doing if the situation was reversed and you had died?

CASE STUDIES

Mary resigns herself to celibacy
Mary and Rose enjoyed a very satisfying sexual relationship and always slept in the same bed. Once the initial shock of losing Rose begins to wear off, Mary longs to be touched and held. But she doesn't want anyone except Rose, and since Rose isn't there she decides that she must put up with never again enjoying physical contact with another human being.

James plays the field
James feels sure that his confidence and therefore competence will return if he proves himself to be sexually attractive again and he begins to look around for a likely new partner. He tries advertising in the local paper and has several nights out with women who turn out to be willing sexual partners but unsuitable in other ways. Then

in the supermarket he meets one of his old flames and he takes her out to dinner. She seems unwilling to pursue the relationship and when he asks why she says that he hasn't sorted himself out yet after losing Elizabeth and suggests that he see a counsellor. James rightly takes this seriously and makes a telephone call to Cruse.

Janet misses her sex life

Janet misses Leroy terribly, most of all at night. Once the children are asleep she gives into her pain and frequently cries herself to sleep, longing to have Leroy beside her, and to have him making love to her. She knows she can never have sex with him again but she begins to be afraid that she will never have sex with anyone else either. Some days she sees men in the street that she really fancies and she fantasises about going to bed with them. She thinks this is disloyal to Leroy and feels very ashamed of her feelings. She then discovers that masturbation helps her feel less pressurised by her sexual longings.

SUMMARY

1. Some bereaved people feel a desperate sexual need.

2. Some people take advantage of any offers of sex that come their way.

3. Some people decide to remain celibate for the rest of their lives.

4. Everyone has to solve the sex problem in the way that suits them best.

5. It's not necessary to feel guilty after enjoying sex with a new partner.

DISCUSSION POINTS

1. How would you deal with overwhelming sexual feelings after the death of your partner?

2. How important would it be to you to feel sexually attractive?

3. Would you feel guilty about having sex with someone else soon after your partner's death?

6
Dealing with Finances

TAKING RESPONSIBILITY

Most, though not all, partnerships share their financial resources and arrangements. After your partner's death you will have to take full responsibility for your own finances and may have to make major adjustments to the way you do things.

Some of these adjustments can be distressing. If financial problems are pressing, you may not have the luxury of a period of mourning surrounded by familiar things, the opportunity to consider the best possible time to make changes. You may be forced to sell or let your home just at a time when you would rather allow the events of everyday life to wash over you with the balm of familiar shared memories.

Whether or not you have to face such problems will depend on how your finances as a couple were organised, probably in one of the following ways:

1. One partner totally financially dependent upon the other with the dependent partner playing no part in the management of the finances.

2. One partner totally dependent on the other for income, but playing a full part in the management of the finances.

3. Both partners contributing to the income but only one managing the finances.

4. Both partners contributing to the income and managing the finances jointly.

Being a surviving provider and manager
If you have been the one who has provided all the income and managed all the finances, you will find few problems in your new

situation. You will know what your income is and what bills needs to be paid, and you'll be used to keeping all the necessary accounts.

Being a surviving dependant

If you were the dependent partner and never played any part in the management of the finances, things will be very different. For a start, depending on the legal status of the partnership, you may find that you have no income at all, other than your own pension if you are over retirement age.

It's possible that you had neither a bank account of your own, nor a joint account with your partner and provider. In that case, even if you were married or if all the money was left to you, the partner's account will be 'frozen' at death. It may take weeks or months before the processes of probate and inheritance law allow you access to the money.

Bank managers do have the power to release some of this money in cases where they are sure it's going to the right person. But otherwise you will have to apply to your local Benefits Office. The only other course of action is to borrow from friends, and you can't do that for long.

Dealing with your partner's bills

If you are unable to pay the household bills that your partner leaves, such as gas, electricity or telephone, it's unwise to just leave them and hope for the best. You are not responsible for bills that were run up in your partner's name, but unless you or your solicitor explain the situation you can find your services being cut off. If there is money in the bank that will eventually be yours, the bills will be settled out of that and you will get what is left. If there is no money available you must take steps to get yourself an income and transfer all household services into your own name, starting new accounts with the suppliers.

Surviving a financially shared partnership

If you were both contributing financially and shared the management of your financial affairs, you will know what to do. As long as you had joint bank or building society accounts the contents of those accounts automatically become yours after the death. None of that money is part of your partner's estate and none of it can legally be called upon to pay your partner's debts. Your biggest problem will be meeting household bills that don't seem to get any smaller on only a proportion of the income.

Wondering how to manage

If you are not used to checking bank statements, paying monthly bills, writing cheques, keeping track of household accounts, a terrible feeling of panic can take over. You may receive bills that seem to be enormous, and you don't know how often to expect them, whether the amount is normal, or whether there is enough money in the account to pay for them. You need to buy food, to pay bus fares or keep the car going – it's all money going out and where is it to come from?

There are, of course, accountants who can manage all this for you, but they cost money on top of everything else. Organising your own finances isn't difficult or complicated, it simply requires a firm step in the right direction. All you need is an account book, perhaps a pocket calculator, and a couple of hours a month to write everything down and do the necessary sums (see Figures 5 and 6). A knowledgeable friend can also be a help during the early months. You will soon find that you have all the necessary information to make the right decisions and take responsibility for your own financial life.

CLAIMING BENEFITS OR PENSIONS

Knowing what you can claim

Some people know how to work out their entitlements to the last penny, others simply don't know what they can claim until they ask. You can find the address of your local Benefits Office in the telephone directory and there is a Family Credit Helpline (01253 500050).

It can be a daunting prospect to join a queue at the local Benefits Office, but there is an appointments system and once you get to talk to someone you will be given advice, which should be thorough, and forms to fill in.

If you are refused one kind of benefit, you may be entitled to another, and you may be able to claim any of the following:

- A widow's payment (tax-free lump sum for widows under state pension age).

- Widowed mother's allowance (weekly benefit for widows of any age who have one child for whom they get Child Benefit. This doesn't apply to widowed fathers in the same situation and a Campaign for Widowed Fathers' Benefits is currently trying to have the rules changed).

HOUSEHOLD ACCOUNTS
MONTHLY BALANCE

INCOME

State pension	£276.00
Occupational pension (after tax)	£525.00
Interest account	£150.00

Total income   £950.00

EXPENDITURE

Regular outgoings

Gas & electricity	£100.00
Telephone	£30.00
Savings for car tax & service	£100.00
TV licence stamps	£8.00
Standing orders at bank	£120.00
Savings	£75.00

Variable outgoings

Food *etc* at supermarket	£300.00
Other cash shopping (including newspapers & magazines)	£100.00
Lottery	£10.00
Clothes	£50.00
Petrol	£60.00
Entertainment & presents	£50.00

Total spending   £903.00

Fig. 5. Example of household accounts – monthly balance.

ANNUAL SUMMARY

Expenditure		Income
January	£900.00	
February	£905.00	
March	£925.00	
April	£845.00	
May	£940.00	
June	£925.00	
July	£913.00	
August	£960.00	
September	£870.00	
October	£915.00	
November	£1024.00	
December	£1250.00	
Total	11372.00	£11400.00

Fig. 6. Example of household accounts – annual summary.

- Widow's pension (weekly benefit for childless widows aged 45 or over when husband died or when Widowed Mother's allowance stops).

- Social Fund Funeral Payment.

- Social Fund Cold Weather Payment (towards the cost of extra heating in severe weather).

- Social Fund Maternity Payment (to help buy things for a new baby).

- Social Fund Community Care Grant (to help in special circumstances with travel costs and other expenses).

- Social Fund Budgeting loan or Crisis loan (loans to meet important or crisis expenses).

- One parent benefit.

- Guardian's allowance (if you are bringing up a child that isn't yours but for whom you are legally responsible).

- Retirement Pension.

- Incapacity Benefit (if your married partner died as a result of industrial injury or disablement).

- Income support (if your income is below a certain level).

- Child Benefit.

- Family Credit (an allowance for working families with children).

- Housing Benefit (for help with paying rent).

- Council Tax Benefit (reduced payments for those on low incomes).

- Various disability benefits.

Advice on pensions can be obtained by telephoning the Pensions

Office (0191 203 0203). They won't give you information about how much money you will be entitled to, but they will tell what you can claim for and send you the necessary forms to fill in.

Someone new to all this may find it easier to begin at a Citizens' Advice Bureau where all the necessary information is brought together by sympathetic advisers.

CLAIMING LIFE INSURANCE

If your partner has left life insurances, either standing on their own or attached to a mortgage on your home, you or your partner's executor need to inform the insurance companies concerned about the death as soon as possible. This is easy enough if your partner has always kept their affairs in order and the information about these policies is readily available. However, sometimes policies don't come to light for weeks or even months after the death, when personal papers are being sorted out.

The insurance company will require to see an original Death Certificate, which is a copy of the entry in the Register of Deaths, issued by the Registrar. You will probably also have to fill in a claim form and send in other certificates, such as your own birth certificate, to prove that you are the person entitled to claim the insurance.

All the certificates will be returned to you once the insurance company has completed its records and if there are no queries the money will be paid out promptly.

INHERITING MONEY OR PROPERTY

Inheriting when there is a Will

Any inheritance resulting from the death of your partner will be dealt with by the executor named in your partner's Will, which may be you. It is the executor's job to sort out the payment of all outstanding debts, including that of the funeral director, and to make sure that any remaining property or money goes to the person or people entitled to them.

When there is a Will there is usually no problem deciding who should have what. The only exception to this is if a dependent partner or child is left without any kind of share of the inheritance. If this is the case, the Will can be challenged in court, but before starting this kind of action it's best to consult a solicitor or the Citizens' Advice Bureau.

Inheriting without a Will

If your partner died intestate, which means there was no Will, you can apply to the Probate Office (England and Wales) or the Procurator's Office (Scotland) for permission for you or your solicitor to act as executor.

In this situation your right to inherit anything depends on the legal status of the partnership. If you were married, you have the right to continue to live in the family home and to a share of all property and money with your partner's children.

You may still be able to keep the home and some of the money if you weren't married but the partnership was what is called a 'common law' marriage, which means that you were publicly recognised as living as a married couple for a number of years. You also have a claim if you have children from the partnership to bring up. However, being a 'common law' partner isn't recognised in law and you would have to go to court to establish your claim, so you would need the help of a solicitor.

If you had a partner of the same sex you aren't recognised by inheritance law either, even if you were totally dependent on your partner for income. In this case the only way your partner can provide for you after death is to make a Will.

MAKING ENDS MEET

Charles Dickens, who knew a lot about debt, wrote:

> 'Annual income twenty pounds, annual expenditure nineteen nineteen six, result happiness. Annual income twenty pounds, annual expenditure twenty pounds ought and six, result misery.'

David Copperfield

This still holds true today and if you are one of those who are unfortunate enough not only to lose your life partner but to find yourself having to cope on a reduced income, you will have to take immediate action to avoid getting into debt. The options are:

- reducing your expenditure

- increasing your income

- finding someone else to support you.

Reducing your expenditure

This is never comfortable because it involves changes in lifestyle that most people would prefer not to make.

When you are on your own some things cost you less, some cost you more and others stay about the same.

For example you will spend **less** on:

- groceries
- clothing
- entertainment
- Council Tax
- public transport.

You may spend **more** on:

- telephone
- household help – cleaning, maintenance, gardening.

You will probably spend about the same on:

- rent or mortgage
- insurances
- water
- fuel
- motoring.

Looking at these lists will give you some idea of the areas where you may be able to cut down on your spending.

You may be able to make the necessary reduction by changing to a smaller car, buying fewer clothes, taking cheaper holidays, not going to expensive restaurants or shows, taking the children away from their private school.

On the other hand you may have to take more drastic action such as moving to a cheaper home, which may be in a neighbourhood you don't like. You may have to do without a car altogether, buy your family's clothes in jumble sales, not have a holiday at all, apply for free school meals for your children, never have an evening out.

Increasing your income

You may have the skills, the time and the energy, and be of an age, when you can increase your income. This may simply involve being able to get a job whereas previously you had none, or working longer hours at what was a part-time job.

You may have entrepreneurial skills and be able to develop a business of some kind which would not only bring in extra money but would give you a new challenge in a life that you are trying to start over again.

You may earn enough extra cash by enterprises such as car boot sales, making desserts for restaurants, sewing, carpentry, running a mobile video library. The list of possible ideas is varied and interesting. The main thing to be careful of is that you really are making a profit, which isn't the same thing as the cash you are taking in. You should also keep careful accounts for the Inland Revenue because sooner or later they are bound to want a slice of what you make.

Letting rooms

If you have enough space in your home to take in lodgers, you may like to consider renting out rooms. Under the Inland Revenue's 'Rent a Room' scheme you can earn up to £62.50 a week from lodgers without paying any extra tax.

You will have to consider carefully whether you would find the presence of strangers in your home unduly intrusive. It may be, of course, that you are able to rent to people you know and you will welcome the company. It may be that you start out hoping for the best and later find that the whole thing was a mistake.

If you are renting to strangers make sure they are reliable and trustworthy. It's perfectly reasonable to ask for references from employers and previous landlords. To ensure they don't end up owing you rent or doing damage to your property it's also reasonable to ask for a deposit of up to three months' rent in advance, to be repayable when they leave, with proper notice and providing they have done no damage to your property.

It's as well to be businesslike about references and deposits even if you are renting to friends, because you won't be entering into this kind of arrangement as a favour to anyone. If friends are reluctant to be businesslike in return then perhaps you should ask yourself whether they are trying to take advantage of your situation and whether you can't find someone more suitable to share your home.

Running a B&B

You may prefer to use your extra rooms to run a Bed & Breakfast business if there is a demand for this type of accommodation in your area. You would have to comply with various rules and regulations which vary according to the number of guests you would be taking in at any one time. You would find out about these by contacting:

- your local Fire Department
- the Inland Revenue
- your Council Tax Department
- your local Environmental Health Department
- your insurance company.

You would also, by law, have to keep a Visitor's Book.

Finding someone else to support you

In Victorian times, when middle-class women were not expected to have jobs, a widow would normally have to find a new husband to support her as soon as possible after her bereavement.

Nowadays, a bereaved person of either sex is generally frowned upon if they admit they are looking for a new partner because they need the income. But there are people who do just that and it has to be admitted that the resulting partnerships are often successful and happy. This is an option which certainly shouldn't be ruled out, especially if you are a person with a lot to offer in exchange for financial support.

CASE STUDIES

Mary gets in a muddle

Mary has never been much good with money and she always left the financial management to Rose. They had a joint bank account so she has no immediate difficulty after Rose's death, but bills and bank statements throw her into a panic and she often pushes them into a drawer without opening them. Before long she doesn't know how much money she has or what she owes.

Rose's brother took her Will away with him, saying he would deal with it, and eventually Mary receives a letter from a solicitor saying that the brother is challenging Mary's right to remain in their joint home, or to use any of Rose's money. Mary is very upset, knowing that she and Rose shared everything and left everything to each other. She goes to a solicitor who tells her that the brother has no case – as the survivor of joint ownership Mary would have rights to the house and bank account even if Rose had left no Will. Realising that she is in a financial muddle, the solicitor recommends an accountant to sort out her affairs.

James has no financial problems

Although James has to manage on a single state pension after Elizabeth's death, he has no worries because he still has a substantial occupational pension and he owns his own home. A life insurance policy pays for Elizabeth's funeral. She had her own bank account which she used for her allowance and personal bills but there is less than a hundred pounds in it. Everything else was in James' name. He congratulates himself on managing his finances so well until his bank manager asks him to think about the difficult financial position Elizabeth would be in if he had died first.

Janet claims all her allowances

An adviser at Janet's bank has made sure she has claimed her widow's payment and her widowed mother's allowance. At first she was worried about the cost of the Kids' Club but she finds that with her allowance, and with not having to budget for food and clothes and entertainment for Leroy, she can just about manage to pay for the Club and keep their standard of living on the same level as before. Because she is concerned about providing long-term security for the children she takes out an extra life insurance policy and enquires about applying for promotion in her job in order to earn more money.

SUMMARY

1. Some people are more used to dealing with finances than others.

2. People who have left the financial management to their partner have to get to grips with their new situation.

3. People who have been financially dependent on their partner may be left without an income.

4. A sole-name bank or building society is 'frozen' on the death of the signatory.

5. A joint account, or jointly owned property, automatically passes to the surviving signatory or owner.

6. If your partner didn't make a Will you may not be entitled to inherit anything.

DISCUSSION POINTS

1. Are you satisfied that you are managing your financial affairs in the best possible way?

2. If you have to cut down on spending, what can you do without?

3. If you want more money coming in, what can you do about it?

4. Are you sure you are getting all the pensions and allowances you are entitled to?

7
Restructuring Your Life

LOSING A SHARED LIFE

Being part of someone else
When a relationship develops into a permanent partnership of some kind, you and the other person evolve into a single unit. The changes taking place will have been so slow and subtle that at the time neither of you may have been aware of them. But in time you'll have been able to anticipate each other's thoughts and needs without speaking; you'll have known your partner's attitudes so well that you could voice them yourself.

In fact, you will have become as familiar with your partner's personality as with your own.

All this, which grew so slowly and gradually, is snatched away suddenly and brutally, and it's only when the shared life has gone for ever that you realise just how strong were these inter-twining bonds.

Now you are going to have to rebuild your personality and your life so that you can function again on your own. You are going to have to become an independent person.

Regaining independence
You can't go back to the way you were before you met your partner and shared your life, nor would many people want to. What you shared with your partner will be part of the person you will be in the future. But that person will also incorporate something new, something that is exclusively you.

That something may well come from your past. It may well be the determination to survive, the memory that you were once an independent person before you met your partner and can therefore be so again.

For example:

- If you have spent years as a home-maker and carer, did you once have a job that interested and absorbed you? Did you earn your own living and meet all your own financial needs?

- If your partner always did the shopping, cooking and laundry, wasn't there a time when you ironed your own clothes and fixed your own meals?

- If you always let your partner do the driving, didn't you once drive yourself? Or aren't you now as capable as anyone else of learning to drive?

- If you left the management of your finances to your partner, didn't you once have a bank or savings account of your own? If so, then ask yourself why it is so frightening to do so again.

MAKING CHANGES

Deciding when to change

Some people think that after losing your partner you should make changes to your life as quickly as possible, to help you to get over your loss. They think that living in the same surroundings will only make it harder for you to recover.

Others believe that sticking to what is familiar will help you through the first rocky period when you will find it very hard to cope with each new day. During this time even the most decisive person may find it difficult to make decisions about their future.

The truth is that everyone is different. Although there are recognisable patterns, everyone reacts differently to the loss of a partner and what may be the right thing for you will be the wrong thing for the next person. You will have to take events as they come and if you really can't bear to be alone in the familiar surroundings, you must make changes quite quickly. If, on the other hand, you feel that you need time to relive the old times in peace, then you must make that time if you can.

Deciding what to change

When Winston Churchill had important decisions to make, he would list the possible pros and cons of each side of the argument, to help him to see the situation more clearly.

This idea can be adapted to help in the long and daunting journey back to independence.

For example:

- Make a list of all the things your partner used to do that you will have to do for yourself in the future. Underline the things that you

MARY'S ACTION PLAN

LIST 1
THINGS ROSE USED TO DO
Accounts & bills
Arrange insurance
Book holidays
Car service & MOT
Arrange household repairs
Lock up at night
Deal with spiders

LIST 2
THINGS I HAVE TO DO DIFFERENTLY
Work on Rose's biography
Keep the lodgers happy
Cook proper meals
Keep track of the keys & lock up
Learn to look after the car
Learn to manage my money
Remember to put out the rubbish
Plan my holidays

LIST 3
THINGS I WOULD LIKE TO CHANGE
Get a cat for company
Make less work in the garden
Find someone to go out with
Starting painting again
Go shopping in a more convenient
    supermarket
Watch less intellectual TV programmes
Get a smaller car

LIST 4
THINGS I DON'T WANT TO CHANGE
The house and its contents
Rose's books

IN 1 MONTH	IN 3 MONTHS	IN 6 MONTHS	IN 1 YEAR
Lock up properly	Look after the car	Arrange household repairs	Arrange a holiday
Work on the biography	Shop in a more convenient place	Get a smaller car	Change the garden
Cook myself proper meals	Watch the TV that that I like	Understand the insurance	Find someone to go out with
Look after the lodgers	Manage the money	Get a cat	
Put out the rubbish		Starting painting again	

Fig. 7. Example of action plan.

will have to learn to do from scratch.

- Make a list of the things you used to do but will have to do differently now.

- Make another list of all the things that don't *have* to be changed but you would like to do differently now.

- Finally list the things you would like to keep as they are.

Now start on a fresh sheet of paper and divide it into four columns, with a heading for each of 1 month, 3 months, 6 months, 1 year.

Finally, take each item from your first three lists and allocate it to one of the time columns. Probably the most important will have to be done sooner but you may include in the first two columns things that aren't urgent but really seem attractive to you, like learning to sail or going to Tibet.

When you've finished you will have an action plan for restructuring your life, and you will find increasing satisfaction, as the months pass, in ticking off the items you have achieved (see Figure 7).

But don't forget, nobody is perfect, and there may be things you don't manage to get to grips with. All you have to do is to move these things back into a longer time-scale, or find a reason why they no longer need to be done.

CONSIDERING MAJOR CHANGES

Some of the changes you have listed may be minor matters such as those mentioned in Chapter 4. But others may be major, irrevocable changes in your life or your surroundings.

You may have decided to:

- move house to a new neighbourhood

- move to a new city

- get a new job

- start a business

- go travelling

- start a course of study

- clear the cupboards of your partner's possessions.

Any of these require careful thought and organisation, and as much help as you can get from other people.

Moving house

You may decide to move for a number of reasons:

- You have a new job that is too far away from your home.

- You want to get away from the memories of your shared life.

- You want to be nearer to members of your or your partner's family.

- You want to be further away from members of your or your partner's family.

- You want a change of social scene.

- You don't need so much accommodation now that you are on your own.

- You have always wanted to live in a different environment but couldn't because your partner was against it.

Once you have made up your mind you will have to face up to dealing with estate agents, solicitors and removal firms. If you're not sure that you can do this on your own, try to arrange for a friend always to be present at important meetings.

And never be on your own when prospective new owners or occupants are looking around your home, or when you are looking around with a view to choosing your new home, because you are particularly vulnerable in these situations. The estate agent should always be willing to accompany you, but you must remember that, however friendly they seem, they have a vested interest in making a sale and may persuade you into a deal against your better judgement. In other words, while you should be able to count on their help it's unwise to expect them automatically to be on your side.

Coping with reawakened memories

When all the arrangements have been made and the time comes to move, you are likely to feel especially distressed. Even for people who haven't been bereaved, moving house is one of life's most stressful periods. For you, packing up the little items that have made up your shared home will sharpen all your memories again. It may even be that if you are moving to a smaller place you will have to sell some of the furniture that you bought together over the years. You need to be prepared for the deep emotions that may be aroused.

Once in your new home you will have so much to occupy you that you may go for days without thinking about your partner at all. As well as organising your home the way you want it, you will need to familiarise yourself with a new neighbourhood, get to know new people, concentrate on making that fresh start you have promised yourself.

Starting a new job

If a new job is your way of making ends meet financially, you will probably be putting yourself under a lot of extra pressure that you don't really need. It's stressful even filling out an application form, wondering if your skills and achievements match what the employer is looking for. Then, if you are successful in achieving an interview, you have the stress of trying to make the right impression and finally waiting for the result.

When you finally manage to land a job you will have a whole new range of pressures to cope with. Just getting to work on the first day can be a draining experience requiring careful planning. Getting through the first week and month in an unfamiliar workplace can make the burden of the job seem almost too much and you will wonder if you are going to be able to cope, especially if you haven't been out to work for some time.

Remember that this stress isn't peculiar to your situation as a bereaved person – everyone finds it difficult to start in a new job.

Whatever your reasons for making the change you will be stimulated by the new opportunities open to you. You will be free to take lunch with colleagues or socialise after work because it no longer matters that you do the shopping or arrive home at a certain hour. You will be able to start again with a fresh slate in an environment where you are not regarded as 'Poor so-and-so, whose partner died'.

Starting a business

This can be challenging and difficult at any time of life, but if you are sure of your ability to cope with long hours of work and have the necessary financial backing, it can be the surest road to independence.

Anyone contemplating such a course should understand that it is never as easy as it looks to be your own boss. Those who do it successfully know their business inside out from the start. They do thorough market research and take sound professional advice at every stage.

There's plenty of help available. Every major bank has its own business advisory service and there are numerous consultants and publications ready to help you – for a price. You can also get help through your local Job Centre.

Travelling

People who have tried this say it has done a lot to re-build shattered self-confidence. It takes a lot of courage to travel as a single person after being part of a couple, but some people find that joining a tour or making a journey, long or short, is a good way of taking a fresh look at the outside world and at themselves. For one thing, you may see sights and meet other people that make you feel your situation is not so terrible after all. For another, you will certainly meet people who know nothing about what has happened to you and once again you will be able to escape the 'Poor so-and-so' attitude.

Studying

You may decide to prepare yourself for your new life by doing a course of study, either to refresh and expand your skills and interests or to gain new qualifications. There are many different qualifications to aim for, and a number of routes to each of them, according to your circumstances and the time you have available (see Figure 8).

Your local sixth form college or adult education centre will have a wide variety of courses for part-time study at many levels. Or you may choose to study through a correspondence centre such as the Open University, the Open College of the Arts or the National Extension College.

Clearing the cupboards

It's difficult to know when to do this. Some people like to get rid of everything that reminds them of their dead partner as soon as possible, and say that it makes them feel better.

Others have said that they like to keep clothes and other possessions because just to touch something that still has the feel and smell of the dead partner is comforting. Bereaved people often find it comforting to wear their partner's clothes.

Sometimes a house move or the start of a new relationship signals that it's time to have clear out and if you've kept everything you will have to make hard decisions, sometimes face up to having old wounds opened. One widow has written about the difficult decision she made to give all her partner's academic books to a university library. Another found that she could part with everything except

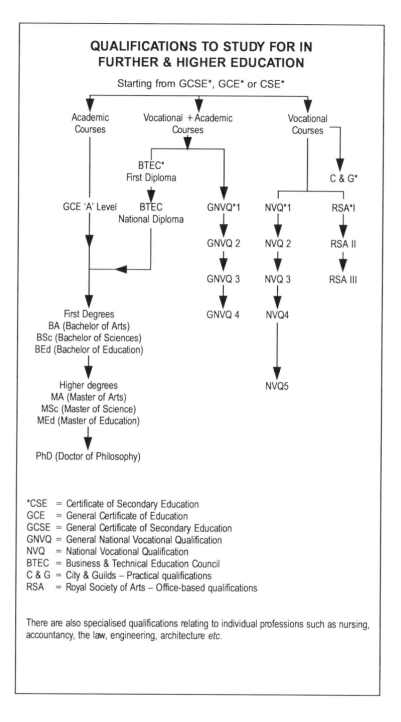

Fig. 8. Further and higher education qualifications (England and Wales).

her partner's woodworking tools and lived for years with chisels that he had carefully and lovingly sharpened, and boxes of screws with the sizes carefully marked up in his handwriting.

Making your own choices

Inevitably, contemplating many of these changes will bring an initial feeling that what you are about to do may be disloyal. You won't be helped by those friends and family members who will tell you that it isn't good for you to be making such changes, even though there are others who will have been suggesting for months that you should be putting your past life behind you.

There is nothing disloyal about realising that you are ready to move on in life. This is perfectly normal and it would be unhealthy if you did otherwise. The timing is a matter for your choice, not for the advice of others.

APPRECIATING FREEDOM

There is a film called *Truly, Madly, Deeply* about a young woman grieving after the death of her partner. After a few weeks she is granted the dearest wish of anyone who mourns, her partner returns to her, as a ghost, to live with her once again.

At first they are ecstatically happy, then things begin to go wrong and it dawns on her that even in the short time since his death she has begun to change into a different person. She is already moving on into her own life and they no longer get along as well as they did. In the end she has to tell him to go and they part company, amicably enough but with a great deal of relief, each to follow their own new paths.

This is what happens to all of us when we start out on our own in the same situation.

Acknowledging that you have moved on

As time passes, it does no harm to stop and reflect from time to time, to try to imagine you and your partner doing together whatever you are doing alone at that moment. The chances are that more and more the picture will become incongruous. You will shake your head and realise that he or she might not understand what you are doing or why you are doing it, might feel emotionally threatened by what you are able to achieve on your own, might have tried to stop you doing whatever it is.

And at first you may feel guilty about this.

But there is no need. What is happening is not a sign that you are forgetting your partner, that you are devaluing his or her memory in any way. It is a sign of healthy recovery on your part. You are gaining a new freedom and this should be appreciated and enjoyed.

CASE STUDIES

Mary takes in lodgers
Even after the solicitor and accountant have reassured her, Mary is still very worried about money, believing she will never be able to pay all the bills from her own pension. Then when the new university term begins Josephine mentions that she and a friend are looking for new digs and Mary has the idea of letting a couple of rooms to them. Although she doesn't consciously want to change anything in the house from the way Rose liked it, having the young people about forces her to reorganise some of the rooms and rethink some of her routines.

James rearranges his life
James finds it hard to talk to his bereavement counsellor at first, but after a few sessions he begins to recognise that his guilt feelings are irrational because, apart from the times when he tried to leave her, which was many years ago, he never told Elizabeth that he wanted to be rid of her. As he talks things through he begins to remember how much he did to please her, including living in a house that he never really liked. This makes him decide to move and he chooses a new place in the country, with a bigger garden. He enjoys redecorating it according to his own tastes. He remembers, too, that he once wanted a dog but Elizabeth would never agree to it, so he goes to the RSPCA shelter and picks a young mongrel. He is so busy with his move that he hasn't time to continue seeing his counsellor.

Janet is given opportunities
Janet is offered training with a view to promotion to an assistant manager's job. However, this means going away from home for the course and then moving to another area to work in a larger branch. She hesitates because she doesn't want to upset the children's lives. But then she remembers how much her parents wanted to help her so she talks it over with them and they agree to look after the children while Janet does her training, then to help her with her house move. Janet is worried that the move will unsettle the children

again, but she asks them to help her to make decisions about the way things are arranged in the new house and they seem to take it all in their stride. With a guilty start she finds herself enjoying making decisions without having to consult Leroy and try to please him all the time.

SUMMARY

1. Learning to manage without your partner means growing into a different, independent person.

2. Making a definite action plan can help you to restructure your life.

3. There are many changes, major and minor, that you can choose to make.

4. The timing and nature of the changes you make are up to you, not other people.

DISCUSSION POINTS

1. Would you find it easy to assume your independence? What would you have to learn to do for yourself?

2. What sort of points would be priorities in your Action Plan?

3. Would you find a move to a new home or a new job stimulating or too stressful to contemplate?

4. How do you feel about the task of clearing out your partner's personal belongings?

8
Finding New Interests

STAYING PUT

You may shudder at the thought of some of the drastic changes and challenges outlined in the last chapter. There may be all sorts of good reasons why they aren't for you. However ready you feel to move on into a new life, you may be either unable or unwilling to change your job or your home.

Perhaps you don't want to change your home because:

- You prefer to live amongst memories of your relationship with your partner.

- You are quite content where you are and know that you would be unlikely to find a place anywhere else that suits you so well.

- You have children whose school careers would be disrupted by a move.

- You know that a move would only add to your feelings of insecurity.

Perhaps you don't want to change your job because:

- It is a job you thoroughly enjoy and you have worked hard to get to your present position.

- You earn a salary that you couldn't hope to equal if you started again elsewhere.

- You enjoy the company of your colleagues and have happy relationships with them that you wouldn't want to lose.

- You have children and your work has been arranged to fit around their needs.

- You are nearing retirement and your age and pension arrangements make a change either difficult or unwise.

Whatever your reasons, you are going to stay put, but you still feel that need for new independence, you want to make changes in your life.

DOING SOMETHING DIFFERENT

Finding out about things
One of the strengths of life in Great Britain is that whatever your interests you can be sure that:

1. Within a few miles there will be a group of like-minded people formed into an association or society that you can join.

2. There will be a library where you can ask for information to help you to follow that interest.

The exceptions to this are people who live in far-flung rural areas, or on small offshore islands. But nowadays there is always the Internet, providing you can afford to link yourself up.

The point is that, whatever you may choose to do to expand or change your life, you should be able to find a ready-made group waiting to welcome you.

Trying things out
If you're not sure what you want to do, a glance down the list of adult education classes in your local library or the 'What's On' section of your local newspaper will provide plenty of ideas. If you're not sure whether you're going to get on with, say, stamp collecting or horse-riding, the only course of action is to try them both out. You can always give them up if you find that they don't suit you.

Your choice of activities may be limited by the fact that you have children who take up a lot of your leisure time, or you haven't any spare cash for fees and equipment. You will find that there are some things, like walking or gardening or painting, which need cost little or nothing and which you can do with your children. And many activities have reduced fees for pensioners or families on benefit.

Volunteering
You may also be able to contribute to voluntary activities such as charity fundraising, helping out at your local animal shelter, helping with reading at your local school, hospital or hospice visiting, helping the National Trust, and many other things which will truly

cost you nothing and which can be fitted around the needs of a family.

If you are constantly dashing out to different meetings or classes, you'll soon find yourself so busy that your friends will wonder what has become of you. It might be easy to over-commit yourself and become tired and stressed but it doesn't have to stay that way. After a while of trying out this and that you will soon know what suits you and what doesn't, and be able to work out a routine accordingly.

TAKING HOLIDAYS

Holidaying alone
Some people are happy to plan and take a holiday on their own. They really enjoy their own company and the freedom to do exactly what pleases them each day without considering the needs of another person.

The disadvantage is that the holiday will probably be more expensive for a single person than for two people sharing, because many hotels and holiday companies add on a 'single supplement' for guests occupying alone a room for which the holiday company has budgeted to receive two tariffs.

Another disadvantage is the possibility of becoming a target for other people on their own, looking for a companion to spend the time with. Sometimes good friendships are formed in this way, but the other person may not necessarily be the sort you will get along with and it can be very difficult to shake off an unwelcome would-be companion staying in the same hotel.

And however much a person likes their own company, it can be very hard in the newly-single state to see other couples all around, enjoying being together. All the old feelings of anger and resentment may come flooding back and while these may not last for long, they could end up spoiling the holiday.

Holidaying in groups
There are specially organised 'singles' holidays where people can book up on their own in the knowledge that when they arrive at their destination they will immediately be a part of a ready-made group of friends.

That is certainly one option for some bereaved partners who fall within the age group specified by the organisers (usually under 30) and are ready to accept that there may be strong sexual overtones built into the holiday's activities.

There is also the option of special group holidays centred around specific activities. There are tours of gardens and stately homes, for example, and a single person would fit very well into a pony trekking holiday, or a sailing trip organised by one of the many sailing schools or sail training ships. Many hotels also run off-season 'Activity Weeks', catering for special interests, where single people are welcomed. This kind of holiday is always advertised in the magazines related to the special interest.

More information about holidays for single people, including those with no single supplement, can be found in the Cruse publication *Holiday Ideas*.

Sharing your holiday

Some people like to share their holiday with another single or bereaved friend. These kinds of arrangements can work well, but they can be full of pitfalls and it's as well to lay down some basic ground rules first.

For example:

- Do you both like doing the same kinds of things with your time? If not, would you be content to lie on the beach by yourself while your friend climbs a mountain, or vice versa?

- Do you both enjoy the same kinds of restaurants?

- Do you both intend to spend roughly the same amount of money on extras, or will you find yourself paying more so that your friend can join in some of these activities with you?

- What will happen if your friend behaves like Shirley Valetine's friend – goes off with someone he or she fancies and leaves you to fend for yourself?

- What happens if you meet someone you like the look of on the first day and you want to spend time with him or her? Will your friend be upset or just shrug and go off alone?

It's unwise to make assumptions about any of these things, however well you think you know the person you are going on holiday with. Try talking them over first. If this causes arguments, better to have them before you go away than let them spoil an expensive holiday that should be relaxing.

DEALING WITH CRITICISM

Whatever new activities you feel like trying out, don't be put off by the reactions of other people when you announce your intentions. This seems to be another area in which our friends and families seem to think they know better than we do what is going to be good for us. Some of the responses you may hear are:

- You'll never be able to manage that!

- Didn't you try that once and give it up?

- That doesn't sound very suitable!

- Isn't that rather dangerous?

- Won't that be too difficult?

- Won't that be too expensive?

- Won't that take up rather a lot of time?

- But that's only for men/women!

- Aren't you a bit old for that?

These negative comments can be very irritating but you shouldn't let them worry you. One very effective response is to ask the person concerned to come along with you. You don't have to be newly bereaved to benefit from trying out new activities.

CASE STUDY

Mary signs up to study

Having some extra money coming in gives Mary more confidence. While she is working in the university library she notices an advertisement for a course with the Open College of the Arts. Before she met Rose she was considered quite a promising water colourist and she has been thinking about taking it up again. She sends for the information and enrols for a fine art course.

SUMMARY

1. You may want to try out new interests and there are plenty of things to choose from.

2. If you've found you don't like an activity, or you haven't time to

do everything, you can always give something up.

3. Holidaying alone brings special problems but there are solutions.

4. Friends and family may try to put you off doing new or unusual things.

DISCUSSION POINTS

1. Have you a mental list of activities you would like to try?

2. Would you be put off by people telling you an activity isn't suitable for you for some reason?

3. What kind of holiday would suit you best now that you are on your own?

9
Forming New Relationships

LOSING YOUR FRIENDS

In losing their partner, some people lose the only real friend in their lives.

And some find that, because they are no longer part of a couple but have become a single person, they lose the friends that they shared with their partner as sets of couples. It may seem unbelievable that anyone could be so insensitive as to push a newly-bereaved person out of their circle of friends, but that's exactly what seems to happen on may occasions.

When you become a single person again after losing your partner the way the rest of the world relates to you changes almost overnight. At first you may be far too engrossed in your grief and the immediate practical problems of life for it to matter to you, but gradually you will realise what is happening.

Being excluded

At first you may find that you are invited out as before with a 'spare' partner provided for you by a thoughtful hostess, much to the embarrassment of you both. But before long it's likely that you simply won't be invited at all. This syndrome doesn't have to be limited to the dinner party set. If your social life involved meeting up in the pub with pairs of friends, or going on days out with other couples, the chances are that before long you will soon get the message that things have now changed and you no longer fit into the group.

There are several reasons for this, and they don't all mean that your friends are being insensitive. It can be that:

- They don't know what to say to you or how to deal with your grief. Therefore it is less painful for them if you aren't there.

- They understand that for a while you won't want to go out, then as time passes the group changes and there is no place for you.

- You are seen as a sexual threat. Once you are single you may be seen as a predator and therefore a competitor. You may not have any such thoughts, but the partners of your friends will.

- You are changing. Working through your grief and learning to manage on your own, your interests and concerns are different and you no longer have so much in common with your former friends. You will feel this as much as they do.

People recall how devastated they were when they found themselves dropped by couples they used to be friends with when their partner was alive. One widow writes of being bluntly told that she reminded her friends too much of her dead husband, so they didn't want to spend time with her any more.

MAKING NEW FRIENDS

Unless you are a real loner, you will want to have friends about you, so if you have lost your old friends you will have to go about making new ones.

There is a difference between making friends and meeting new acquaintances. If you move to a new job or a new area, or try out some of the activities outlined in the last chapter, you will soon find that you have met a wide circle of new people. However, not all of them will necessarily be new friends.

Meeting acquaintances

Acquaintances are people you know but don't necessarily spend time with. They may be people met at work, in the hairdresser's or the local shop, at an evening class.

You may get to know quite a lot about these people – where they live, how old they are, what they do for a living – but never feel enough empathy with them to want to deepen the relationship into friendship.

Most of the people we come across in life become acquaintances rather than friends, because friendship is something more special.

Having friends

We all have different definitions of friendship but most people would agree that it is something deeper, more emotionally satisfying, more involving than acquaintanceship. A friend is someone you relate to easily, someone you feel you can ask for help, someone you would give help to without begrudging your time. A friend is someone you can talk to without fear that you will be judged or your confidence will be betrayed, someone you can laugh with and cry with, someone you spend time with by choice.

Some of our friends are people we have known for years and perhaps hardly ever see except for special occasions, but we know they are always there. Some of our friends are people we see every day of the week – perhaps we meet them for lunch, go shopping together, go out with them in the evening.

Finding friends

As you recover from your bereavement and become a new person you may feel the need to make new friends, but this won't be easy when you carry with you the emotional baggage of such a devastating loss. You can't begin a prospective friendship by burdening someone you don't know very well, but would like to know better, with the story of your loss. That presumes too much, or gives too much of yourself away too soon, and can well be off-putting to the other person. Yet eventually they are going to find out what has happened to you and then they will wonder why you didn't tell them and feel that perhaps you aren't becoming such a good friend as they thought.

There is no easy answer to the finding and making of friends. It's something we all do in our own way and in the end the friendships that become most precious to us are those based on a gut feeling about the other person.

The only certainty is that you will need to find ways of making new friends after your loss. If you don't, if you shut away the inner self that we all give to our friendships, you may not be able to grow and develop naturally through the rest of your life.

FORMING NEW PARTNERSHIPS

There is another aspect of your new life that will be separate from making changes to your job or your home, finding new interests or making new friends. This is the very private matter of embarking on a new partnership.

Looking for a new partner

The time comes when you have gone through the process of mourning, made all the changes you want to and started out on your new life, and you begin to think that it would be nice to have someone to share it with. Sometimes this thought occurs only because you have met someone you think might be suitable.

But sometimes the thought comes first, when you look around you and consider that you are missing out on something important by living a single life.

So where do you find this person who will meet your expectations, be available and unattached, and eventually love you back?

Much depends on your age, of course. If you are still on the young side of 40 there will still be available people around, moving in and out of the web of relationships that makes modern life. But once you approach your 50s potential partners are thin on the ground.

You may meet someone through one or other of the new activities you are trying out. You may meet someone in your new job, or on holiday. You may find that you have known and been admired for most of your life by someone who is just waiting for the appropriate moment to declare themselves to you.

Finding someone by accident

Perhaps you don't make a conscious decision about looking for someone, you simply meet a person you like the look of, who is free and returns your interest, and away you go.

This can be the least complicated way of starting a new relationship but it is unlikely to be as simple as it was the first time around, for a number of reasons:

1. Because you are older and wiser this time you will probably stop and ask yourself a few pertinent questions if an apparently suitable partner appears in your life. For example, if this person is unattached what has prevented them forming a steady relationship with someone else?

2. It may be that the person is in the same state as you – they have had a beloved partner who has died. In that case you will both have to learn to shoulder part of the other person's emotional luggage from the old relationship. You will have to learn not to be offended if you hear mention of the way the past partner used to do things, not to mind your new partner telling you about the old one – after all, the last relationship was a big part of their life and they can't be expected to shut the door on it.

3. You will have to learn to establish yourself, not try to be an imitation of your predecessor, and not to expect your new partner to do things the way your last partner used to.

4. You will have to consider the feelings of your children, especially if they are not yet grown up.

5. Your potential new partner's own children may resent you
    when you try to take the place of their missing parent.

However, if you take things gently and carefully you will
gradually grow together and the past relationships will impinge
less and less on the new ones, but be prepared for some tricky
moments in the meantime.

FALLING IN LOVE AGAIN

It is by no means necessary to fall in love in order to begin a new
relationship. Many very happy partnerships develop through a
gradual deepening of friendship, especially the second time around,
when the people concerned are more mature.

But, as so many people know, age is no protection against that
amazing obsession known as falling in love. It can happen to
octogenarians as easily as to teenagers.

The problem is that while society is prepared to be tolerant of the
behaviour of teenagers in love, it is often less understanding about
parents and grandparents mooning around, leaping to the
telephone, walking around hand in hand, kissing in public, making
opportunities to go to bed together.

If this is you, you may find that your children or friends will tell
you that you are making a fool of yourself.

This can be very hurtful, especially if you were hoping that they
would feel happy for you. If it is accompanied by advice that you
stop seeing so-and-so because he or she is totally unsuitable for you,
you may feel very uncomfortable indeed.

It may make you look afresh at the person you are in love with
and find that the advice has some foundation, that you have been
blinded by your feelings. Or you may laugh it off as an amusing role
reversal, reminding your children that this is exactly how you felt
about them when they were courting.

You may be able to take heed of what is being said, making
allowances for the fact that a potential new partner may make your
family feel insecure, but let your love affair take its natural course.

DEALING WITH DISAPPOINTMENT

That natural course may lead in the end to tears and disappointment. Every time we commit ourselves to a new relationship we take
that risk and the more intense the feelings are, the greater the

disappointment and pain if we are let down.

Just as falling in love is not the prerogative of the young, neither is falling out of love, running around with more than one person at a time, changing your mind and falling for someone else instead, running away from steady commitment.

Whatever the plot of the love story when the participants are young, it can equally apply to mature lovers. If we want to play the game we must remember that our feelings and pride are at stake, and be stable enough to survive losing. After all, if you have fallen in love again once, it can happen to you twice.

MAKING A NEW COMMITMENT

Supposing everything has gone well with your new relationship, you and your partner are content with each other's company, you are sexually compatible, your families get on well enough. It is time to make the final commitment of sharing a home and a bank account.

There will be several major decisions to make:

- Will you marry or cohabit?

- Will you want separate bedrooms?

- Whose home will you live in, or will you buy a new place between you?

- Will you keep your finances separate and just combine for the housekeeping, or will you put everything together?

- When you set up housekeeping together, who is to pay for what?

- Do you know how much each of you expects to spend on food, drink, clothes, entertainment, the home and the garden?

- If you are combining all your assets, how are you going to provide for your children's inheritance?

- If you are keeping your assets separate, do you intend one another to inherit, or your children?

If it sounds as though there is more emphasis here on money than love, remember that most of the rows that married couples have are about money. So it seems sensible to discuss some of the points of potential dispute before the partnership is finalised, so that any assumptions and misapprehensions can be settled in good time.

After that you have every chance of settling down to a long and happy relationship.

CASE STUDIES

Mary is making the most of her life

One day Mary realises that she is actually enjoying her new life, working on the biography, cooking for her student lodgers and studying art. On the course she meets people who know nothing about her past life and when a group get together to go on a painting holiday in Italy the following summer, Mary joins them. She wonders whether she is being disloyal to Rose's memory, but she has the feeling that Rose is never far away and is approving of what she is doing.

James makes new friends

In his new home James finds it difficult to continue seeing his old friends, but he joins several clubs and activities in the nearby villages and meets many new people. He soon finds himself attracted to a widow who runs the village pub and he can't believe his luck when she seems to feel the same way about him.

Janet wants a new man

Janet is very busy with her new home and her new job, and trying to be both parents to her children. She misses her friends from her old home but she has no time to socialise and meet new people, though she does manage lunch with a couple of colleagues once a week. Sometimes she finds herself suffering aches and pains and crying with exhaustion in the evenings after the children are in bed. She has read some books on bereavement and decides that she is suffering from post-traumatic stress. She considers contacting Cruse to see a counsellor but decides that what she really needs is a new relationship to make her feel like a human being again. She has no feelings of guilt about this because she knows it's what Leroy would have wanted for her. She begins to make a list of all the places where she might meet someone suitable (see Figure 9).

SUMMARY

1. It isn't uncommon to lose the friendship of other couples after your partner has died.

2. New friends can be found through new activities or work.

3. For many people the time comes when they are ready to

WHERE TO MEET A NEW PARTNER

THE SUPERMARKET – seen a dishy fellow but I'll have to go without the kids if I'm to chat him up.

THE KIDS' SCHOOL – join the PTA.

THE NEIGHBOURHOOD – keep my eyes open and never pop down to the shop looking less than perfect.

ADULT EDUCATION – join a car mechanics or woodwork class, sure to be full of interesting men.

FRIENDS – Angie from the lunchtime group at work was dropping hints about meeting her cousin.

WORK – might be distracting, even disastrous if it goes wrong.

HOLIDAY – by myself or with the kids.

Fig. 9. Janet's list of possible places to meet a new partner.

consider finding a new partner.

4. Falling in love is just as much fun and just as complicated the second time around.

5. Anyone setting out on a new relationship may have to deal with the disapproval of their family.

6. Anyone considering making a new partnership a permanent arrangement should consider all the implications carefully beforehand.

DISCUSSION POINTS

1. Would you be really hurt or would you understand if your 'couple' friends stopped seeing you?

2. Are you the sort of person who finds it easy to make friends or do you find that most of the people you meet remain as superficial acquaintances?

3. What sort of qualities would you look for in a new partner?

10
Remembering

LIVING WITH YOUR MEMORIES

As time goes by it will become obvious that the people around you expect you to banish your memories of your dead partner, as part of the process of 'getting over it'. For a while friends will be sympathetic, they will try to make life easier for you and be prepared to listen when you want to talk about your partner. But before long you will become aware that they are listening with slightly fixed, polite little smiles and you will know it's time to keep your thoughts to yourself.

Many people believe that the main objective of the bereaved is to forget about the person who has died. Time, they think, heals all things. They have heard it said so often that it must be true and there is no reason for them to know any better.

The reality is that time is not so forgiving. It only allows you to get used to all things. You may be able to get along with your grief at losing your partner, you may grow away from what you were when you shared your life and begin a satisfactory new life for yourself, but you will never forget. You will always remember how it was and what you had together. And that's the way you will want it.

Remembering the good times

These memories will become increasingly important. It may be hard to believe, but you can eventually begin to forget what your partner looked like, what their voice sounded like. You can use your memories like a photograph album, to help you to stay close, to remind you of what you used to laugh about together.

At first you will find that you have very mixed recollections. Good and bad days bring good and bad memories and on some days the bad come flooding back more easily than the good. But if your life together was a normal balance between happy and not-so-happy times, you will find that the happy memories eventually predominate.

TRYING TO FORGET

Some people have no happy memories. If you are one of those, if your life with your partner was hell from beginning to end, you will want to escape from the past, but you will find it just as difficult as a person with happy memories. The times may become less frequent when you wake up in the morning expecting to find your partner still beside you, when you experience a stab of guilt because you have done something that wouldn't be approved of, but it will never stop happening.

This is because your memories, good and bad, are a part of what you are. You can do your best to shut them away, to refuse to let them get through to the present, but they are always there. To understand this is to be able to defend yourself against being taken over completely by unwelcome memories which, if they won't go away, can have a disastrous effect in the long term.

Ways of defending yourself are:

- leading a busy life

- talking to someone who has more to be unhappy about than you do

- getting rid of objects, such as a particular household ornament or piece of furniture, that trigger the memories

- planning to be especially busy at the time of anniversaries.

ESTABLISHING FORMAL MEMORIALS

Most people are content to follow convention and have a gravestone or a memorial in a crematorium garden which acts as their last remaining point of contact with the mortal remains of their partner. This can act as a focal point for the expression of love and respect as anniversaries come around. Anniversaries can also be publicly marked by 'Memoriam' notices in local newspapers.

But there are other ways of establishing memories. Some can be very simple such as the red ribbon or badge devised by Red Ribbon International and worn in memory of people who have died of HIV/AIDS. Or you might favour something more elaborate. Your partner may not have an airport or space station named after them unless they are as famous as John F. Kennedy or Martin Luther King, but anyone who has given some kind of public service might well merit a public park or building.

It is not essential to have money for this. Of course, if you are wealthy it makes a noble and important gesture to set aside a capital sum as a Trust Fund, but many people without a penny to their name have set out to raise money in memory of their loved ones which has then been the basis of a memorial trust fund. Such a fund can be used for:

- a piece of equipment for a local hospital

- a research project

- awards for scholars and artists

- travel bursaries for young people

- third world development projects

- a literary prize

- a sports hall

- a school prize.

The list of possibilities only comes to an end when the imagination runs dry.

For example, Susan Elliott, widow of actor Denholm Elliott, set to work to raise money for a memorial fund with which she established a respite home for people suffering from HIV and their carers.

Anyone wanting to set up a memorial fund should contact a solicitor who specialises in trusts. Solicitors in your area can be obtained by telephoning the Law Society in London or by consulting the *Law Society Regional Directory*, held in major public libraries or Citizens' Advice Bureaux.

BUILDING POSITIVE MEMORIES

Remembering publicly

As the first anniversary of your partner's death approaches you will find that you receive invitations from the crematorium, the hospice or hospital, the cemetery authorities, to take part in services of remembrance. You may find these fairly informal public occasions helpful in reminding you to mark the time. However, they can also be fairly meaningless and it's as well to remember that they are organised not only to help the bereaved but also to raise the profile of the institution concerned and thus to bring in much needed funds.

Remembering privately

Many people prefer to establish their own private memorial rituals, or to have none at all, simply remembering as and when it seems appropriate to them.

Whichever type of memorial you adopt, without a doubt it will change its form as your needs change. At first you may visit the grave or garden of remembrance regularly. Then when you find yourself busy, or have to move away, or you form a new relationship, your visits will become less frequent. This doesn't mean that you are forgetting about your partner, simply that your memories are taking a different form.

Editing your memories

As you move through your grief and begin to rebuild your life you may also begin to edit your memories, so that the past seems rosier than it really was, rosier than anyone's past ever can be.

There's no harm in doing this, it's natural and positive to build up the good memories and stop harping on the bad ones that may still cause anger and resentment. But don't be surprised if, sometimes, you find yourself stopping short in the middle of a little reverie and saying firmly to yourself, 'Surely it was never like that!'

Whatever it was like, it was different from your present situation. In one way always a part of you, in another irretrievably relegated to the past, your relationship with your partner was unique, personal to you alone. Your memory of that relationship will also be personal, your own to do with as you want, not as other people may judge to be correct.

CASE STUDIES

Mary establishes a memorial fund

When Rose's estate is finally sorted out Mary's accountant is able to tell her that she has quite a large sum of money at her disposal. Mary decides to establish a trust fund in Rose's memory to help students at the university. This will coincide with the publication of the biography and there is a special memorial ceremony at the university. Mary is happy to take part but she realises that the clever and respected 'public' Rose is someone very different from her own beloved partner, whose memory she will always keep strictly to herself.

James prefers to forget

James has worked hard at freeing himself from the memory of Elizabeth and after his move he has kept nothing of their life together except for a few photographs. He still makes the journey back to the cemetery every now and again, to check that her grave is in good order, but it's only out of a sense of duty.

Janet keeps the good times alive

Janet often talks to the children about Leroy and shows them photographs so that they won't forget him as they grow up. She does her best to remind them of the happy times they had together and when she finally finds a new partner she doesn't hesitate to talk about Leroy to him as well. But they never go back to the crematorium garden where Leroy's ashes are buried because none of them feel that the place has any connection with the person they loved.

SUMMARY

1. People will expect you to want to forget about your dead partner.

2. Your memories will always be important to you.

3. Some people need to keep their memories at bay.

4. There are many different kinds of formal memorial.

5. Many people decide to keep their memorials informal and private.

DISCUSSION POINTS

1. How would you react to a friend who constantly wants to talk about a dead partner?

2. How would you cope with unwelcome memories?

3. What kind of memorial would you like for yourself after you have gone?

Discussion Points:
Suggested Solutions

CHAPTER 1

1. This isn't easy because people in that situation feel that they would prefer to die than to carry on, but they manage it by concentrating on one day at a time.

2. For the first few days a sort of a natural anaesthetic takes over, making it easier to deal with these things. However, what is really needed is a reliable and helpful friend.

3. There is no certain way but by writing a Living Will setting out all their wishes, and lodging it with their doctor and solicitor, a person can make it clear that when they die they want their partner to be included in all decisions.

4. Be patient, but firm. However, don't forget that you may need their help before long. Try saying something like 'I know you are trying to help but just at the moment what I need most is to be left alone. I'll call you later.'

CHAPTER 2

1. The best thing is to be there to listen when they want to talk about their pain, however often they tell you the same story. Some practical help like shopping or child-minding is also useful but don't interfere if your friend says everything is all right.

2. Try to talk to them. Put your arms around them. Let go and cry on their shoulder.

3. It may be possible to do things to help people along by planting

ideas in their minds, but the whole grieving process is so unpredictable that planning just doesn't come into it.

4. Again, you can only plant the idea and leave the appropriate literature lying around. The counselling will only be really effective if the bereaved person wants it enough to make the contact for themselves.

CHAPTER 3

1. It's not really possible to *make* a child understand anything. Whatever you tell them, they will put their own interpretation on events and only slowly come to see the death for what it really is. Don't force things, just tell the truth every time you are asked.

2. Starting a relationship with another partner is a very personal decision. But everyone needs to be special so consider whether it's fair to expect a new partner to be a substitute for the one who has gone.

3. The only social life some parents want is to be with their children. Others would end up being very depressed and boring parents if they weren't able to go out with their friends from time to time.

CHAPTER 4

1. You could ask them. And you will probably find that if you stick around too long it will become pretty obvious that it's time to go.

2. Everyone's list is different. It's surprising what you can forget when you are trying to get back to normal after a bereavement.

3. Would your partner really have minded you making changes?

CHAPTER 5

1. Whether you decide to bottle up your feelings or to have a wild fling with someone, you won't be the only person who has done the same.

2. Different people have different priorities about this, but it can be the start of a downward spiral in self-confidence if you think nobody ever fancies you.

3. Well, would you? Why?

CHAPTER 6

1. You may be very competent at this sort of thing but there's always room for improvement and it does no harm to review what you are doing.

2. When you are used to spending on certain things it's often difficult to see where you can cut down. Why not sit down and talk it over with a friend, and make a list of what you can really do without?

3. The easiest thing is to look for a job but there are lots of ways of increasing your income from home. Why not start by making a list of those you think might suit you?

4. If you don't know where to begin, make an appointment with your local Citizens' Advice Bureau. You'll find the number in the telephone directory and the staff are specially trained to deal with problems like yours.

CHAPTER 7

1. The most frightening part of this is the thought of managing alone. When you have made up your mind that you must learn about the things your partner used to do, you'll find you're more capable than you thought.

2. You won't know until you make the effort to sort it out.

3. The trouble is that you probably won't find the answer to this until it's too late to change your mind. That's why it's better not to make this kind of move too soon after your partner's death so that you have plenty of time to think and to prepare for it.

4. It's always painful to do this but it can be comforting, too, to

handle the things that bring back happy memories of your time together.

CHAPTER 8

1. Go on, we all have. Even if they sound like pure fantasy, why not give yourself the fun of thinking about them?

2. Perhaps it would be wise to give it a second thought because they might be right. But they might also just be envious.

3. There are a lot of options to choose from but perhaps you should try to avoid one where you will be likely to meet only with other couples.

CHAPTER 9

1. People say that they have found this one of the worst experiences to cope with after their bereavement. On the other hand, you may decide you have nothing more in common with friends who would do such a thing.

2. Friendship is a very personal thing. Some people like to surround themselves with people they can relate to, others are happy with only one or two.

3. Why not write a wish list? But remember that you may fall in love with someone who doesn't fit in with your list at all but would still make a good partner.

CHAPTER 10

1. The only friendly thing you can do is listen for however long it takes.

2. There is no way of making yourself immune to bad memories, but you can prevent them from taking you over by avoiding the situations that bring them on.

3. There are a lot of possibilities but don't make it too difficult for your survivors!

Glossary

Academic. To do with theory and books.

Advance Directive. See Living Will.

Apathy. A feeling of not caring enough to do anything.

Benefits Agency. The government department that allocates various welfare allowances.

Bereavement. The loss of something or someone dear or important.

Bereavement counsellor. A counsellor trained to help people with bereavement problems.

Burial. Disposing of a body by burying.

Celibacy. Not having any sexual relationship.

Certificate of Cause of Death. The Certificate issued by a doctor attending a death.

Chapel of Rest. A chapel or similar room where bodies are placed, usually while in the care of a funeral director, after they have been laid out in their coffin.

Clinical depression. A severe form of depression caused by physical or emotional problems that cannot be shaken off without treatment.

Cohabitation. An unmarried couple living together as though they were married.

Coroner. The official responsible for conducting inquests in England, Wales and Northern Ireland.

Counselling. A form of therapy which aims to heal emotional problems by allowing the afflicted person to talk about what they are feeling.

Counsellor. A person who provides counselling.

Common law marriage. A couple who have been living together and are publicly accepted as being husband and wife. This relationship has no legal status under modern law.

Cremation. Disposing of a body by burning.

Death Certificate. The Certificate issued by the Registrar which is a certified copy of the entry in the Register of Deaths.

Dependants. The people who depend on another person, usually financially.

Depression. A feeling of being miserable and low in spirits.

Emotional. Something relating to the feelings of a person.

Entrepreneurial skills. Skills in setting up and running a business.

Executor. The person who undertakes the responsibility of proving a Will and carrying out its instructions.

Extra-marital relationship. A sexual relationship between two people who are not married.

Heterosexual. A person sexually attracted to a person of the opposite sex.

Homosexual. A person sexually attracted to another person of the same sex.

Infant school. School for children between 5 and 7 years old.

Inland Revenue. The government department responsible for collecting taxes.

Intestate. Dying without leaving a Will.

Junior school. School for children between 8 and 11 years of age.

Life insurance. An insurance policy that pays out a sum of money on the death of the person insured.

Living Will (also known as an Advance Directive). A document setting out a person's wishes about medical treatment and the circumstances surrounding their death.

Memoriam notices. Advertisements in a newspaper or magazine commemorating the date of a person's death.

Mortuary. A place where dead bodies are kept.

Next of kin. The nearest living relative by blood or marriage.

Nursery school age. Children between 3 and 5 years old.

Practice counsellor. A professional counsellor who works from a health centre or doctor's practice.

Probate Office. The Office responsible for proving that a Will is valid and giving the executor permission to carry out its instructions.

Procurator Fiscal. The official responsible for conducting inquests and public prosecutions in Scotland.

Promiscuous. Being sexually active with a number of people at the same time, or in quick succession.

Psychological. Something relating to the mind.

Physical. Something relating to the body or the measurable laws of nature.

Significant adults. The adults who hold an important place in a child's life.

Single supplement. A surcharge made by hotels for a single person occupying a room or apartment intended for two or more people.

Trust fund. A capital sum of money legally arranged so that the interest on it must be used for a particular purpose.

Vocational. Practical skills and training directly relating to an occupation.

Voluntary activities. Work undertaken without pay.

Further Reading

CHAPTER 1

Bereavement, Help the Aged.

Dealing with a Death in the Family, Sylvia Murphy (How To Books, 1997).

What to do after a death in England and Wales, Benefits Agency D49 (HMSO, 1995).

What to do after a death in Scotland, The Scottish Office.

What to do when someone dies, Paul Harris (Consumers Association, 1994).

CHAPTER 2

After the death of someone close, Caroline Morcom (Cruse Bereavement Care).

A grief observed, C S Lewis (Faber & Faber, 1961).

All the days ahead, Freda Baker (Darton, Longman & Todd, 1992).

The courage to grieve, Judy Tatelbaum (Cedar Books, 1981).

Through grief: the bereavement journey, Elizabeth Collick (Darton, Longham & Todd, 1986).

Widow's journey: a return to living, Xenia Rose (Condor – Souvenir Press, 1990).

You'll get over it: the rage of grief, Virginia Ironside (Hamish Hamilton, 1996).

CHAPTER 3

A child's grief, Julie Stokes and Diana Crossley (Broadcasting Support Services, Channel 4 Television).

Caring for bereaved children, Mary Bending (Cruse Bereavement Care).

If you have children: some practical advice for widowers, Susan

Walbank (Cruse Bereavement Care).

CHAPTER 4

Household guide for widowers, Susan Walbank (Cruse Bereavement Care).

Living alone (Cruse Bereavement Care).

CHAPTER 5

The empty bed: bereavement and the loss of love, Susan Walbank (Darton, Longman & Todd, 1992).

CHAPTER 6

Benefits Agency leaflets:
  FB2 – *Which benefit?* 1997
  FB27 – *Bringing up children?* 1997
  FC1 – *Family Credit Claim Pack* 1996
  SB16 – *A guide to the Social Fund* 1996
  D49S – *What to do after a death in Scotland: Social Security Supplement 1995*
How to Claim State Benefits, Martin Rathfelder (How To Books, 1995).
How to Start a Business From Home, Graham Jones (How To Books, 1994).
Inland Revenue leaflets:
  IR45 – *What to do about tax when someone dies*
  IR87 – *Letting and your home*
  IR91 – *A guide for widows and widowers*
  IR92 – *A guide for one-parent families*
Managing Your Personal Finances, John Claxton (How To Books, 1996).
Putting your affairs in order: five simple steps to peace of mind in later life (Age Concern).
Taking in Students, Rosemary Bartholomew (How To Books, 1996).
The Which? guide to giving and inheriting, Jonquil Lowe (Consumers Association, 1996).

CHAPTER 9

Friendship, sex and remarriage (Cruse Bereavement Care).

Useful Addresses

BEREAVEMENT SUPPORT

Cruse Bereavement Care, Cruse House, 126 Sheen Road, Richmond, Surrey TW9 1UR. Tel: (0181) 940 4818 and 18 South Trinity Road, Edinburgh EH5 3PN. Tel: (0131) 551 1511.

Jewish Bereavement Counselling Service, PO Box 6748, London N3 3BY. Tel: (0181) 349 0839.

Lesbian and Gay Bereavement Project, Vaughan M Williams Centre, Colindale Hospital, London NW9 5HG. Tel: (0181) 200 0511. Helpline (0181) 455 8894.

London Association of Bereavement Services, London Voluntary Sector Resource Centre, 356 Holloway Road, London N7 6PN. Tel: (0171) 700 8134.

National Association of Bereavement Services, 20 Norton Folgate, London E1 6DB. Tel: (0171) 247 1080 (referrals); (0171) 247 0617 (administration).

National Association of Widows, 54–57 Allison Street, Digbeth, Birmingham B5 5TH. Tel: (0121) 643 8348.

Sudden Death Support Association, Chapel Green House, Chapel Green, Wokingham, Berkshire RG40 3ER. Tel: (0118) 979 0790.

LIVING WILLS

Natural Death Centre, 20 Heber Road, London NW2 6AA. Tel: (0181) 208 2853.

Terrence Higgins Trust, 53–54 Grays Inn Road, London WC1X 8JU. Tel: admin & advice (0171) 831 0330; helpline (noon–10pm daily) (0171) 242 1010; legal line (Mon and Wed 7–9pm) (0171) 405 2381. (Provides counselling, information and advice for people with HIV and their families.)

SINGLE PARENTING

Gingerbread, 16–17 Clerkenwell Close, London EC1R 0AA. Tel: (0171) 336 8183; advice line: (0171) 336 8184; fax: (0171) 336 8185.

Gingerbread Wales, Mansell House, Room 1, 99 Mansell Street, Swansea SA1 5UE. Tel: (01792) 648728.

Holiday Care Service, 2nd Floor, Imperial Buildings, Victoria Road, Horley, Surrey RH6 7PZ. Tel: (01293) 774535; fax: (01293) 784647. (Provides information about suitable holidays for one-parent families, and how to get assistance with the cost.)

Kids Club Network, Bellerive House, 3 Muirfield Crescent, London E14 9SZ. Tel: (0171) 512 2100/2112.

National Council for One Parent Families, 255 Kentish Town Road, London NW5 2LX. Tel: (0171) 267 1361; fax: (0171) 482 4851.

Single Parent Action Network (SPAN), Millpond, Baptist Street, Easton, Bristol BS5 0YW. Tel: (0117) 951 4231.

The Parent Helpline: Tel: (0171) 837 5513. (National helpline giving parents details of childcare in their area.)

FINANCE

Benefits Agency, DSS, Washington, Newcastle upon Tyne NE88 1AA. Tel: 0800 441144 for advice on filling out claim forms.

Family Credit, Family Credit Unit, DSS, Government Buildings, Penwortham, Cop Lane, Preston PR4 0BR. Helpline: (01253) 500050.

National Debtline, Birmingham Settlement. Tel: (0645) 500 511.

The Campaign for Widowed Fathers' Benefits, 15 Whiteway Close, St George, Bristol BS5 7QZ.

SOCIAL SECURITY PUBLICATIONS

HMSO, The Causeway, Oldham Broadway Business Park, Chadderton, Oldham OL9 9XD.

The Scottish Office Home Department, St Andrews House, Edinburgh EH1 3DG. Tel: (0131) 244 3458.

DEALING WITH A WILL

Principal Probate Registry, Somerset House, Strand, London WC2R 1LP. Tel: (0171) 936 6983/7464.

The Commissary Office, 27 Chambers Street, Edinburgh EH1 1LB.
   Tel: (0131) 225 2525 Ext 2253.
The Master, Probate & Matrimonial Office, Royal Courts of Justice
   (Northern Ireland), PO Box 410, Chichester Street, Belfast BT1
   3JF. Tel: (01232) 235111.

LEGAL ADVICE

Solicitors Family Law Association (SFLA), PO Box 302, Orping-
   ton, Kent BR6 8QX. Tel: (01689) 850227. (Send SAE for a list of
   local solicitors specialising in Family Law.)
The Law Society, 113 Chancery Lane, London WC2A 1PL. Tel:
   (0171) 242 1222.

MEMORIALS

Red Ribbon International, The Gatehouse, City Cloisters, 188–194
   Old Street, London EC1V 9FR. Tel: (0171) 216 0106; Fax: (0171)
   216 0107.

Index